THE COMPILERS

BARRY LAZELL and DAFYDD REES are directors of the Media Research And Information Bureau (MRIB), a company which exists to provide a service for many areas of the music industry. MRIB currently compiles charts, airplay information and release listings for several publications, including Music & Video Week, Record Business, Video Business and Popular Video. It also contributes to Sounds and Flexipop, and is currently working on future titles to be published by Virgin Books.

MRIB has also been responsible for the origination and co-ordination of the HMV Shop/Radio 1 Easter Marathon Pop Quiz; and the further work in the broadcasting field with London's Capital Radio.

Prior to forming the company, Barry and Dafydd were both founder members of the Record Business research department, having previously worked individually for Decca Records, Motown Records and Sounds.

Barry is married, and lives in the middle of Essex with his wife, two daughters and thousands of records. Dafydd is single, resident in London, and also lives amongst several tons of vinyl.

WITH THANKS

The compilers would like to thank several people without whose efforts this book would probably not be in your hands now: Marilyn and Alan, who both gave valuable assistance; Robert Devereux for his patience; Mick Keats, for whom it became almost a labour of love as it was for us; Fred Dellar; the many record company press officers who opened their photo files; and the authors whose earlier books of reference provided in many cases a basis for our own further research, notably Joseph Murrells, Joel Whitburn, Fred L. Worth, and the 'British Hit Singles' team of Jo and Tim Rice, Mike Read and Paul Gambaccini.

Charts and chart positions referred to are in virtually all cases taken from reference to the compilers' own file of 'master charts', an amalgamated assessment of the individual charts published by Billboard and Cashbox in the USA, and by NME, Meldody Maker, Disc, Music Week, Record Mirror and Record Business in the UK. We thank all these publications individually.

The photographs illustrating the book were begged and borrowed from a variety of sources, as well as from MRIB's own photo files. We would like to acknowledge the help of many record company press offices, notably those at Decca, CBS, Polydor, EMI, RCA, Stiff, Motown, Phonogram, United Artists and Chrysalis. Some of the early photos are obviously the work of photographers whom we should credit individually but have no way of identifying. Our thanks and apologies go to these anonymous helpers. Most of the memorabilia and printed matter photographed for illustration comes from the MRIB files; these originate from an even wider range of sources than the photos. Finally, several pictures of Buddy Holly, Cliff Richard, the Everly Brothers, Lonnie Donegan and some other late 50s stars are the copyrights of John Beecher, and again used with thanks.

KU-486-517

CONTENTS

INTRODUCTION

We hope that this book is set out in such a way as to speak for itself and really need very little by way of an explanatory introduction. The aim was simply to offer both informative and interesting (and occasionally amusing) facts, feats and trivia concerning records and the people who make them. We have tried to cover the usual 'who did', 'when was', 'how many', and 'where did' areas in a succinct and readable fashion by means

Buddy Holly & The Crickets

of annotated listings, and we have paid particular attention to 'who did it first' and 'who did it the most' categories, probably the source of the most disagreements and wagers between people who follow rock and pop with any degree of historical interest.

This is a book which you can pick up and put down, skim through or read from cover to cover, without at any time losing your way in a thick tome of text. If you tire of reading about which singles sold the most copies in Britain during the 1950s, go right ahead and read about artists who titled themselves 'Big' or 'Little' because they were proportionately large or small. It's intended to be a fun book as well as an informative one; do go and have fun with it.

Barry and Dafydd, MRIB

SECTION 1

FIRSTS

THE FIRST TEN SINGLES TO ENTER THE UK CHART AT NUMBER ONE

1 **JAILHOUSE ROCK**
   Elvis Presley
   (Jan. 25th 1958 – 4 weeks at No. 1)

2 **I GOT STUNG/ONE NIGHT**
   Elvis Presley
   (Jan. 24th 1959 – 5 weeks at No. 1)

3 **MY OLD MAN'S A DUSTMAN**
   Lonnie Donegan
   (Mar. 26th 1960 – 4 weeks at No. 1)

4 **IT'S NOW OR NEVER**
   Elvis Presley
   (Nov. 5th 1960 – 9 weeks at No. 1)

5 **SURRENDER**
   Elvis Presley
   (May 27th 1961 – 4 weeks at No. 1)

6 **THE YOUNG ONES**
   Cliff Richard
   (Jan. 13th 1962 – 8 weeks at No. 1)

7 **I WANT TO HOLD YOUR HAND**
   Beatles
   (Dec. 7th 1963 – 5 weeks at No. 1)

8 **CAN'T BUY ME LOVE**
   Beatles
   (Mar. 28th 1964 – 4 weeks at No. 1)

9 **A HARD DAY'S NIGHT**
   Beatles
   (Jul. 18th 1964 – 4 weeks at No. 1)

10 **I FEEL FINE**
   Beatles
   (Dec. 5th 1964 – 6 weeks at No. 1)

The release of Presley's 'Jailhouse Rock' single in 1958 marked the first occasion on which the British record industry had to deal with really phenomenal advance orders (over 250,000) followed by equally huge demand over the counter. Release had to be delayed for a week to allow the pressing plant to cope, and when the record hit the shops, almost half a million were sold in three days. Small wonder that it set a new precedent by entering that week's chart at No. 1.

'Jailhouse Rock's advance order figure was successively topped by several of the other records on this list; Presley's own 'It's Now Or Never' (475,000), Cliff Richard's 'The Young Ones' (524,000), and the Beatles' 'I Feel Fine' (750,000), 'I Want To Hold Your Hand' (950,000), and 'Can't Buy Me Love' (over 1,000,000). The last figure is still the record advance order for a single in the UK.

Subsequent entries at number one included several more Beatles singles – 'Ticket To Ride', 'Help', 'We Can Work It Out' and 'Get Back' – plus Slade's 'Merry Xmas Everybody', and more recently the Jam's 'Going Underground' and 'Prince Charming' by Adam & The Ants.

THE FIRST TEN NUMBER ONE SINGLES HITS OF THE FIFTIES (USA)

Nat King Cole

1 **I CAN DREAM, CAN'T I?**
Andrews Sisters
(on Jan. 6th 1950 – top for 4 weeks)

2 **RAG MOP**
Ames Brothers
(on Feb. 3rd 1950 – top for 1 week)

3 **CHATTANOOGIE SHOESHINE BOY**
Red Foley
(on Feb. 10th 1950 – top for 4 weeks)

4 **MUSIC! MUSIC! MUSIC!**
Teresa Brewer
(on Mar. 10th 1950 – top for 4 weeks)

5 **IF I KNEW YOU WERE COMIN' I'D'VE BAKED A CAKE**
Eileen Barton
(on Apr. 7th 1950 – top for 2 weeks)

6 **THE HARRY LIME THEME (THE THIRD MAN)**
Anton Karas
(on Apr. 25th 1950 – top for 11 weeks)

7 **MONA LISA**
Nat 'King' Cole
(on Jul. 7th 1950 – top for 5 weeks)

8 **GOODNIGHT IRENE**
Weavers
(on Aug. 11th 1950 – top for 13 weeks)

9 **HARBOR LIGHTS**
Sammy Kaye Orchestra
(on Nov. 10th 1950 – top for 2 weeks)

10 **THE THING**
Phil Harris
(on Nov. 24th 1950 – top for 4 weeks)

Surprisingly few of these songs have actually disappeared into the sands of time. Anton Karas' zither-played the 'Harry Lime Theme' from the film 'The Third Man'. It can still be heard on radio in the original versions while songs like 'Mona Lisa' and 'Harbor Lights' have been revived many a time. Most of the artists, though, have vanished into oblivion.

THE FIRST TEN NUMBER ONE SINGLES HITS OF THE SIXTIES (UK)

Cliff Richard with the Everly Brothers

Lonnie Donegan

1 **WHAT DO YOU WANT TO MAKE THOSE EYES AT ME FOR?**
Emile Ford
(on Jan. 2nd 1960 – top for 3 weeks)

2 **WHY**
Anthony Newley
(on Jan. 23rd 1960 – top for 6 weeks)

3 **POOR ME**
Adam Faith
(on Mar. 5th 1960 – top for 2 weeks)

4 **RUNNING BEAR**
Johnny Preston
(on Mar. 19th 1960 – top for 1 week)

5 **MY OLD MAN'S A DUSTMAN**
Lonnie Donegan
(on Mar. 26th 1960 – top for 4 weeks)

6 **STUCK ON YOU**
Elvis Presley
(on Apr. 23rd 1960 – top for 1 week)

7 **CATHY'S CLOWN**
Everly Brothers
(on Apr. 30th 1960 – top for 8 weeks)

8 **THREE STEPS TO HEAVEN**
Eddie Cochran
(on Jun. 25th 1960 – top for 1 week)

9 **GOOD TIMIN'**
Jimmy Jones
(on Jul. 2nd 1960 – top for 3 weeks)

10 **PLEASE DON'T TEASE**
Cliff Richard
(on Jul. 23rd 1960 – top for 4 weeks)

THE FIRST TEN NUMBER ONE SINGLES HITS OF THE SIXTIES (USA)

Eddie Cochran

1 **EL PASO**
   Marty Robbins
   (on Jan. 2nd 1960 – top for 2 weeks)

2 **RUNNING BEAR**
   Johnny Preston
   (on Jan. 16th 1960 – top for 3 weeks)

3 **TEEN ANGEL**
   Mark Dinning
   (on Feb. 6th 1960 – top for 2 weeks)

4 **THEME FROM 'A SUMMER PLACE'**
   Percy Faith & His Orchestra
   (on Feb. 20th 1960 – top for 9 weeks)

5 **STUCK ON YOU**
   Elvis Presley
   (on Apr. 23rd 1960 – top for 4 weeks)

6 **CATHY'S CLOWN**
   Everly Brothers
   (on May 21st 1960 – top for 5 weeks)

7 **EVERYBODY'S SOMEBODY'S FOOL**
   Connie Francis
   (on Jun. 25th 1960 – top for 2 weeks)

8 **ALLEY-OOP**
   Hollywood Argyles
   (on Jul. 9th 1960 – top for 1 week)

9 **I'M SORRY**
   Brenda Lee
   (on Jul. 16th 1960 – top for 3 weeks)

10 **ITSY BITSY TEENY WEENY YELLOW POLKADOT BIKINI**
   Brian Hyland
   (on Aug. 6th – top for 1 week)

Long before the days when there was a consistent two-way traffic of chart-toppers across the Atlantic, it can be seen from these two lists that several American number ones found equal success across the water, but in fact none of the British records shown here made the US charts at all (one of them, Anthony Newley's 'Why', was a cover of a 1959 Frankie Avalon US number one in any case.) Strangely, one of the American records to top in Britain – Eddie Cochran's 'Three Steps To Heaven' – had found no top 100 success in its homeland at all.

One interesting statistic here is that Elvis Presley's 'Stuck On You' (his first post-Army single) reached the top in both countries in the same week, while the record which replaced it – 'Cathy's Clown' by the Everly Brothers – did the same.

13

THE FIRST TEN NUMBER ONE SINGLES HITS OF THE SEVENTIES (UK)

Moody Blues

1 **TWO LITTLE BOYS**
Rolf Harris
(on Jan. 3rd 1970 – top for 4 weeks +
2 in 1969)

2 **REFLECTIONS OF MY LIFE**
Marmalade
(on Jan. 31st 1970 – top for 1 week)

3 **LOVE GROWS**
Edison Lighthouse
(on Feb. 7th 1970 – top for 3 weeks)

4 **I WANT YOU BACK**
Jackson Five
(on Feb. 28th 1970 – top for 1 week)

5 **WANDRIN' STAR**
Lee Marvin
(on Mar. 7th 1970 – top for 3 weeks)

6 **BRIDGE OVER TROUBLED
WATER**
Simon and Garfunkel
(on Mar. 28th 1970 – top for 4 weeks)

7 **SPIRIT IN THE SKY**
Norman Greenbaum
(on Apr. 25th 1970 top for 3 weeks)

8 **BACK HOME**
England World Cup Squad '70
(on May 16th 1970 – top for 2 weeks)

9 **QUESTION**
Moody Blues
(on May 30th 1970 – top for 1 week)

10 **YELLOW RIVER**
Christie
(on Jun. 6th 1970 – top for 1 week)

14

THE FIRST TEN NUMBER ONE SINGLES HITS OF THE SEVENTIES (USA)

Jackson 5

Ray Stevens

1 **RAINDROPS KEEP FALLIN' ON MY HEAD**
B. J. Thomas
(on Jan. 3rd 1970 – top for 4 weeks)

2 **VENUS**
Shocking Blue
(on Jan. 31st 1970 – top for 1 week)

3 **I WANT YOU BACK**
Jackson 5
(on Feb. 7th 1970 – top for 1 week)

4 **THANK YOU (FALETTINME BE MICE ELF AGIN)**
Sly & The Family Stone
(on Feb. 14th 1970 – top for 2 weeks)

5 **BRIDGE OVER TROUBLED WATERS**
Simon and Garfunkel
(on Feb. 28th 1970 – top for 4 weeks)

6 **LET IT BE**
Beatles
(on Mar. 28th 1970 – top for 4 weeks)

7 **ABC**
Jackson 5
(on Apr. 25th 1970 – top for 2 weeks)

8 **AMERICAN WOMAN**
Guess Who
(on May 9th 1970 – top for 3 weeks)

9 **CECILIA**
Simon and Garfunkel
(on May 30th 1970 – top for 1 week)

10 **EVERYTHING IS BEAUTIFUL**
Ray Stevens
(on Jun. 6th 1970 – top for 1 week)

Only two records, by Simon and Garfunkel and the Jackson 5, show here as chart-toppers in both America and Britain, although in fact most of these hits had a healthy two-way traffic, in most cases reaching the top ten across the waves. Exceptions from Britain were Rolf Harris and (surprise) the England World Cup Squad, while in the other direction Sly & The Family Stone missed out completely with 'Thank You', and B. J. Thomas' 'Raindrops' was kept down to a fairly lowly chart position by a very strong-selling cover version from Sacha Distel.

THE FIRST TWENTY AMERICAN SOLO ARTISTS TO TOP THE BRITISH SINGLES CHART

Johnnie R

1 **AL MARTINO**
(Nov. 14th 1952 – with
Here In My Heart)

2 **JO STAFFORD**
(Jan. 9th 1953 – with
You Belong To Me)

3 **KAY STARR**
(Jan. 23rd 1953 – with
Comes A-Long A-Love)

4 **EDDIE FISHER**
(Jan. 30th 1953 – with
Outside of Heaven)

5 **PERRY COMO**
(Feb. 6th 1953 – with
**Don't Let The Stars Get In Your
Eyes**)

6 **GUY MITCHELL**
(Mar. 23rd 1953 – with
She Wears Red Feathers)

7 **FRANKIE LAINE**
(Apr. 24th 1953 – with
I Believe)

8 **DORIS DAY**
(Apr. 16th 1954 – with
Secret Love)

9 **JOHNNIE RAY**
(Apr. 30th 1954 – with
Such A Night)

10 **KITTY KALLEN**
(Sept. 10th 1954 – with
Little Things Mean A Lot)

11 **FRANK SINATRA**
(Sept. 17th 1954 – with
Three Coins In The Fountain)

12 **DON CORNELL**
(Oct. 8th 1954 – with
Hold My Hand)

13 **ROSEMARY CLOONEY**
(Nov. 26th 1954 – with
This Ole House)

14 **TENNESSEE ERNIE FORD**
(Mar. 12th 1955 – with
Give Me Your Word)

15 **PEREZ PRADO**
(Apr. 30th 1955 – with
**Cherry Pink and Apple Blossom
White**)

16 **TONY BENNETT**
(May 14th 1955 – with
Stranger in Paradise)

17 **AL HIBBLER**
(Jun. 18th 1955 – with
Unchained Melody)

18 **SLIM WHITMAN**
(Jul. 30th 1955 – with
Rose Marie)

19 **DEAN MARTIN**
(Feb. 18th 1956 – with
Memories Are Made Of This)

20 **PAT BOONE**
(Jun. 9th 1956 – with
I'll Be Home)

Although Americans did generally tend to dominate the British charts for the first few years of their existence, occasionally transatlantic number one hits which might have been expected to repeat their success in the UK were beaten to the post by local cover versions. Nevertheless, artists like Frankie Laine (whose 'I Believe' was at number one for 18 weeks, an unbeatable record) and Guy Mitchell managed to rack up several chart-toppers. Frank Sinatra's 'Three Coins In The Fountain', however, was surprisingly his only record to reach the top in the UK until 'Strangers In The Night', thirteen years later.

THE FIRST TWENTY AMERICAN SOLO ARTISTS TO TOP THE AMERICAN SINGLES CHART

Gene Autrey

1 **BING CROSBY**
(Oct. 10th 1940 – with
Only Forever)

2 **DICK HAYMES**
(Jul. 15th 1943 – with
You'll Never Know)

3 **AL DEXTER**
(Oct. 21st 1943 – with
Pistol Packin' Mama)

4 **DINAH SHORE**
(Oct. 5th 1944 – with
I'll Walk Alone)

5 **PERRY COMO**
(Sept. 6th 1945 – with
Till The End Of Time)

6 **BETTY HUTTON**
(Feb. 21st 1946 – with
Doctor, Lawyer, Indian Chief)

7 **FRANKIE CARLE**
(Mar. 7th 1946 – with
Oh, What It Seemed To Be)

8 **NAT 'KING' COLE**
(Feb. 7th 1947 – with
**(I Love You) For Sentimental
Reasons**)

9 **ART LUND**
(May 30th 1947 – with
Mam'selle)

10 **PEGGY LEE**
(Mar. 5th 1948 – with
Manana)

11 **MARGARET WHITING**
(Oct. 1st 1948 – with
A Tree In The Meadow)

12 **SPIKE JONES**
(Dec. 31st 1948 – with
**All I Want For Christmas (Is My
Two Front Teeth)**)

13 **EVELYN KNIGHT**
(Jan. 14th 1949 – with
A Little Bird Told Me)

14 **VIC DAMONE**
(Aug. 26th 1949 – with
You're Breaking My Heart)

15 **FRANKIE LAINE**
(Sept. 23rd 1949 – with
That Lucky Old Sun)

16 **GENE AUTRY**
(Dec. 30th 1949 – with
**Rudolph The Red-Nosed
Reindeer**)

17 **RED FOLEY**
(Feb. 10th 1950 – with
Chattanoogie Shoeshine Boy)

18 **TERESA BREWER**
(Mar. 10th 1950 – with
Music! Music! Music!

19 **EILEEN BARTON**
(Apr. 7th 1950 – with
**If I Knew You Were Coming, I'd've
Baked A Cake**)

20 **ANTON KARAS**
(Apr. 21st 1950 – with
The Harry Lime Theme)

The first American charts in the 1940s
were pretty well dominated by the big
dance bands, which is why it took a full
decade for twenty different solo artists to
achieve chart-toppers. Most of the
names here, in fact, were ex-featured
vocalists with big bands, or in some
cases, 'holidaying' on a solo release.
Bing Crosby, the appropriate first name
on the list, continued to have many more
chart-topping hits all through this decade.

17

THE FIRST TWENTY BRITISH SOLO ARTISTS TO TOP THE BRITISH SINGLES CHART

1 **LITA ROZA**
(Apr. 17th 1953 – with
How Much Is That Doggie In The Window?)

2 **DAVID WHITFIELD**
(Nov. 6th 1954 – with
Answer Me)

3 **EDDIE CALVERT**
(Jan. 8th 1954 – with
Oh Mein Papa)

4 **VERA LYNN**
(Nov. 5th 1954 – with
My Son, My Son)

5 **WINIFRED ATWELL**
(Dec. 3rd 1954 – with
Let's Have Another Party)

6 **DICKIE VALENTINE**
(Jan. 1st 1955 – with
The Finger Of Suspicion)

7 **RUBY MURRAY**
(Feb. 19th 1955 – with
Softly Softly)

8 **JIMMY YOUNG**
(Jul. 2nd 1955 – with
Unchained Melody)

9 **ALMA COGAN**
(Jul. 16th 1955 – with
Dreamboat)

10 **RONNIE HILTON**
(May 12th 1956 – with
No Other Love)

11 **ANNE SHELTON**
(Sept. 22nd 1956 – with
Lay Down Your Arms)

12 **TOMMY STEELE**
(Jan. 19th 1957 with
Singing The Blues)

13 **FRANKIE VAUGHAN**
(Jan. 26th 1957 – with
Garden Of Eden)

14 **LONNIE DONEGAN**
(Apr. 12th 1957 – with
Cumberland Gap)

15 **MICHAEL HOLLIDAY**
(Feb. 22nd 1958 – with
The Story Of My Life)

16 **SHIRLEY BASSEY**
(Feb. 28th 1959 – with
As I Love You)

17 **RUSS CONWAY**
(Mar. 28th 1959 – with
Side Saddle)

18 **CLIFF RICHARD**
(Aug. 1st 1959 – with
Living Doll)

19 **CRAIG DOUGLAS**
(Sept. 5th 1959 – with
Only Sixteen)

20 **ADAM FAITH**
(Dec. 5th 1959 – with
What Do You Want?)

The staple diet of most British artists of the elderly and mid-fifties was cover versions of big American hits, and eight of the chart-toppers above fall into this category. Tommy Steele's recording of 'Singing The Blues' actually replaced the American version by Guy Mitchell at the Number One position! The first chart-toppers of essentially British music came with Lonnie Donegan's 'Cumberland Gap' in 1957 (along with his Number One follow-up 'Putting On The Style', the biggest-ever skiffle hit), and the records by the UK's first two real rock teen idols, Cliff Richard and Adam Faith as the decade drew to a close.

18

THE FIRST TWENTY BRITISH SOLO ARTISTS TO TOP THE AMERICAN SINGLES CHART

1 **VERA LYNN**
(Jul. 4th 1952 – with
Auf Weidersehen Sweetheart)

2 **MR ACKER BILK**
(May 19th 1962 – with
Stranger On The Shore)

3 **PETULA CLARK**
(Jan. 23rd 1965 – with
Downtown)

4 **DONOVAN**
(Sept. 3rd 1966 – with
Sunshine Superman)

5 **LULU**
(Oct. 21st 1967 – with
To Sir With Love)

6 **GEORGE HARRISON**
(Dec. 26th 1970 – with
My Sweet Lord)

7 **ROD STEWART**
(Oct. 2nd 1971 – with
Maggie May)

8 **GILBERT O'SULLIVAN**
(Jul. 29th 1972 – with)
Alone Again Naturally)

9 **ELTON JOHN**
(Feb. 3rd 1973 – with
Crocodile Rock)

10 **RINGO STARR**
(Nov. 24th 1973 – with
Photograph)

11 **ERIC CLAPTON**
(Sept. 14th 1974 – with
I Shot The Sheriff)

12 **OLIVIA NEWTON-JOHN**
(Oct. 5th 1974 – with
I Honestly Love You)

13 **JOHN LENNON**
(Nov. 16th 1974 – with
Whatever Gets You Through The Night)

14 **CARL DOUGLAS**
(Dec. 7th 1974 – with
Kung Fu Fighting)

Ringo Starr

15 **DAVID BOWIE**
(Sept. 20th 1975 – with
Fame)

16 **LEO SAYER**
(Jun. 5th 1977 – with
You Make Me Feel Like Dancing)

17 **ANDY GIBB**
(Jul. 13th 1977 – with
I Just Want To Be Your Everything)

18 **NICK GILDER**
(Oct. 28th 1978 – with
Hot Child In The City)

19 **M (ROBIN SCOTT)**
(Nov. 3rd 1979 – with
Pop Muzik)

20 **RUPERT HOLMES**
Dec. 22nd 1979 – with
Escape (The Pina Colada Song)

Until the 1960's it was generally accepted that British artists could never really penetrate the American record market with any degree of consistency. It took the Beatles and the mid-60s 'British Invasion' to change all this, but it still remains a fact that it took until the dawn of the 1980s for 20 different British soloists to achieve a number one single in the USA, with the bulk of these having achieved it during the 70s, after the initial British groups boom had died down. A nice irony, though, is that the first British number one in the States, by Vera Lynn, found its mark on the 4th July 1952 – American Independence Day!

THE FIRST TWENTY AMERICAN GROUPS TO TOP THE BRITISH SINGLES CHART

The Crickets

Johnny Otis

1 **BILL HALEY & THE COMETS**
(Nov. 12th 1955 – with
Rock Around The Clock)

2 **DREAM WEAVERS**
(Mar. 17th 1956 – with
It's Almost Tomorrow)

3 **TEENAGERS featuring FRANKIE LYMON**
(Jul. 21st 1956 – with
Why Do Fools Fall In Love?)

4 **CRICKETS**
(Nov. 2nd 1957 – with
That'll Be The Day)

5 **JOHNNY OTIS SHOW**
(Jan. 4th 1958 – with
Ma, He's Making Eyes At Me)

6 **EVERLY BROTHERS**
(Jun. 28th 1958 – with
All I Have To Do Is Dream)

7 **KALIN TWINS**
(Aug. 23rd 1958 – with
When)

8 **PLATTERS**
(Mar. 14th 1959 – with
Smoke Gets In Your Eyes)

9 **MARCELS**
(May 6th 1961 – with
Blue Moon)

10 **HIGHWAYMEN**
(Oct. 7th 1961 – with
Michael)

11 **B BUMBLE & THE STINGERS**
(May 12th 1962 – with
Nut Rocker)

12 **SUPREMES**
(Nov. 14th 1964 – with
Baby Love)

13 **RIGHTEOUS BROTHERS**
(Jan. 30th 1965 – with
You've Lost That Lovin' Feelin')

14 **BYRDS**
(Jul. 17th 1965 – with
Mr Tambourine Man)

15 **SONNY AND CHER**
(Aug. 28th 1965 – with
I Got You Babe)

16 **WALKER BROTHERS**
(Sept. 25th 1965 – with
Make It Easy On Yourself)

17 **FOUR TOPS**
(Oct. 22nd 1966 – with
Reach Out, I'll Be There)

18 **BEACH BOYS**
(Nov. 12th 1966 – with
Good Vibrations)

19 **MONKEES**
(Jan. 21st 1967 – with
I'm A Believer)

20 **GARY PUCKETT & THE UNION GAP**
(May 18th 1968 – with
Young Girl)

Perhaps because no American group had a British Number One hit prior to Bill Haley & The Comets, most of this list is refreshingly familiar, with almost every title (except probably 'It's Almost Tomorrow' and 'Ma, He's Making Eyes At Me') still a regularly heard Radio Oldie. Several of these records – by The Crickets, Johnny Otis, The Kalin Twins, B Bumble and the Walker Brothers – actually scored higher in the UK, failing to reach No. 1 in their homeland.

THE FIRST TWENTY AMERICAN GROUPS TO TOP THE AMERICAN SINGLES CHART

The Everly Brothers

1 **SONG SPINNERS**
(Jun. 24th 1943 – with
**Comin' In On A Wing And A
Prayer**)

2 **MILLS BROTHERS**
(Oct. 28th 1943 – with
Paper Doll)

3 **INK SPOTS with ELLA
FITZGERALD**
(Nov. 30th 1944 – with
I'm Making Believe)

4 **ANDREWS SISTERS**
(Feb. 1st 1945 – with
Rum And Coca-Cola)

5 **JERRY MURAD'S HARMONICATS**
(Jun. 13th 1947 – with
Peg O' My Heart)

6 **AMES BROTHERS**
(Feb. 3rd 1950 – with
Rag Mop)

7 **WEAVERS**
(Aug. 11th 1950 – with
Goodnight Irene)

8 **LES PAUL AND MARY FORD**
(Apr. 13th 1951 – with
How High The Moon)

9 **CREW CUTS**
(Jul. 28th 1954 – with
Sh-Boom)

10 **CHORDETTES**
(Nov. 24th 1954 – with
Mr Sandman)

11 **FONTANE SISTERS**
(Jan. 26th 1955 – with
Hearts Of Stone)

12 **McGUIRE SISTERS**
(Feb. 2nd 1955 – with
Sincerely)

13 **BILL HALEY & THE COMETS**
(Jun. 29th 1955 – with
Rock Around The Clock)

14 **FOUR ACES**
(Sept. 28th 1955 – with
**Love Is A Many-Splendoured
Thing**)

15 **PLATTERS**
(Feb. 17th 1956 – with
The Great Pretender)

16 **EVERLY BROTHERS**
(Oct. 18th 1957 – with
Wake Up Little Susie)

17 **DANNY & THE JUNIORS**
(Jan. 4th 1958 – with
At The Hop)

18 **SILHOUETTES**
(Feb. 22nd 1958 – with
Get A Job)

19 **CHAMPS**
(Mar. 15th 1958 – with
Tequila)

20 **COASTERS**
(Jul. 19th 1958 – with
Yakety Yak)

In a market dominated first by the big bands in the forties, then by the solo 'personality' artist in the early fifties, it took the advent of rock & roll to really accelerate the progress of group records to the US chart-top – hence 15 years for 20 different groups to reach Number One, but nearly half of them got there during the last five. The list includes six groups of siblings, two duos, one husband-and-wife team (Les Paul and Mary Ford) and one wholly instrumental team (The Champs).

THE FIRST TWENTY BRITISH GROUPS TO TOP THE BRITISH SINGLES CHART

1 **STARGAZERS**
(Apr. 10th 1953 – with
Broken Wings)

2 **LORD ROCKINGHAM'S XI**
(Nov. 22nd 1958 – with
Hoots Mon)

3 **SHADOWS**
(Aug. 20th 1960 – with
Apache)

4 **ALLISONS**
(Apr. 8th 1961 – with
Are You Sure?)

5 **TORNADOS**
(Oct. 26th 1962 – with
Telstar)

6 **JET HARRIS & TONY MEEHAN**
(Jan. 26th 1963 – with
Diamonds)

7 **BEATLES**
(Mar. 2nd 1963 – with
Please Please Me)

8 **GERRY & THE PACEMAKERS**
(Apr. 6th 1963 – with
How Do You Do It?)

9 **BILLY J KRAMER & THE
DAKOTAS**
(Jun. 8th 1963 – with
Do You Want To Know A Secret?)

10 **SEARCHERS**
(Aug. 3rd 1963 – with
Sweets For My Sweet)

11 **BRIAN POOLE & THE
TREMELOES**
(Oct. 5th 1963 – with
Do You Love Me?)

12 **DAVE CLARK FIVE**
(Jan. 11th 1964 – with
Glad All Over)

13 **PETER AND GORDON**
(Apr. 25th 1964 – with
A World Without Love)

14 **FOUR PENNIES**
(May 16th 1964 – with
Juliet)

15 **ANIMALS**
(Jul. 4th 1964 – with
House Of The Rising Sun)

16 **MANFRED MANN**
(Aug. 15th 1964 – with
Do Wah Diddy Diddy)

17 **HONEYCOMBS**
(Aug. 29th 1964 – with
Have I The Right?)

18 **KINKS**
(Sept. 12th 1964 – with
You Really Got Me)

19 **HERMAN'S HERMITS**
(Sept.19th 1964 – with
I'm Into Something Good)

20 **ROLLING STONES**
(Nov. 28th 1964 – with
Little Red Rooster)

The dates here tell a significant story about the changing fortunes of group records in Britain – it took from 1953 until 1962 for five different outfits to reach Number One, whereas the remaining fifteen acts all made it in 1963 and 1964. It's also notable that numbers 2, 3, 5 and 6 on the list are all instrumentals, but that once the Merseybeat era arrived, instrumental groups were completely shouldered aside, in favour of (mainly) vocals-plus-instruments line-ups.

THE FIRST TWENTY BRITISH GROUPS TO TOP THE AMERICAN SINGLES CHART

The Troggs

1 **TORNADOS**
(Dec. 22nd 1962 – with
Telstar)

2 **BEATLES**
(Feb. 1st 1964 – with
I Want To Hold Your Hand)

3 **PETER AND GORDON**
(Jun. 27th 1964 – with
A World Without Love)

4 **ANIMALS**
(Sept. 5th 1964 – with
House Of The Rising Sun)

5 **MANFRED MANN**
(Oct. 17th 1964 – with
Do Wah Diddy Diddy)

6 **FREDDIE & THE DREAMERS**
(Apr. 10th 1965 – with
I'm Telling You Now)

7 **WAYNE FONTANA & THE MINDBENDERS**
(Apr. 24th 1965 – with
The Game Of Love)

8 **HERMAN'S HERMITS**
(May 1st 1965 – with
Mrs Brown You've Got A Lovely Daughter)

9 **ROLLING STONES**
(Jul. 10th 1965 – with
(I Can't Get No) Satisfaction)

10 **DAVE CLARK FIVE**
(Dec. 25th 1965 – with
Over and Over)

11 **TROGGS**
(Jul. 23rd 1966 – with
Wild Thing)

12 **NEW VAUDEVILLE BAND**
(Dec. 3rd 1966 – with
Winchester Cathedral)

13 **FOUNDATIONS**
(Mar. 8th 1969 – with
Build Me Up Buttercup)

14 **BEE GEES**
(Aug. 7th 1971 – with
How Can You Mend A Broken Heart?)

15 **MOODY BLUES**
(Nov. 4th 1972 – with
Nights In White Satin)

16 **WINGS**
(Jun. 2nd 1973 – with
My Love)

17 **PAPER LACE**
(Aug. 17th 1974 – with
The Night Chicago Died)

18 **AVERAGE WHITE BAND**
(Feb. 22nd 1975 – with
Pick Up The Pieces)

19 **BAY CITY ROLLERS**
(Jan. 3rd 1976 – with
Saturday Night)

20 **MANFRED MANN'S EARTHBAND**
(Feb. 19th 1977 – with
Blinded By The Light)

The Tornados' 'Telstar' was really an amazing breakthrough, after twenty-odd years with no British group even approaching the American chart-top (unless you count a borderline case – Kenny Ball with His Jazzmen on 'Midnight in Moscow'). With the advent of The Beatles, of course, the achievement became almost commonplace – but it still belonged to a select few, and as the list shows, it was not until 1977 that 20 different acts equalled it. Manfred Mann (1964) and Manfred Mann's Earthband are completely different groups, although led by the same 'name' – hence the two separate listings.

THE FIRST TWENTY GIRL SINGERS TO TOP THE BRITISH SINGLES CHART

Jackie Trent

1 **JO STAFFORD**
   (Jan. 9th 1953 – with
   You Belong To Me)
2 **KAY STARR**
   (Jan. 23rd 1953 – with
   Comes A-Long A-Love)
3 **LITA ROZA**
   (Apr. 17th 1953 – with
   **(How Much Is That) Doggie
   In The Window?**)
4 **DORIS DAY**
   (Apr. 16th 1954 – with
   Secret Love)
5 **KITTY KALLEN**
   (Sept. 10th 1954 – with
   Little Things Mean A Lot)
6 **VERA LYNN**
   (Nov. 5th 1954 – with
   My Son, My Son)
7 **ROSEMARY CLOONEY**
   (Nov. 26th 1954 – with
   This Ole House)
8 **RUBY MURRAY**
   (Feb. 19th 1955 – with
   Softly Softly)
9 **ALMA COGAN**
   (Jul. 16th 1955 – with
   Dreamboat)
10 **ANNE SHELTON**
   (Sept. 22nd 1956 – with
   Lay Down Your Arms)
11 **CONNIE FRANCIS**
   (May 10th 1958 – with
   Who's Sorry Now)
12 **SHIRLEY BASSEY**
   (Feb. 28th 1959 – with
   As I Love You)
13 **HELEN SHAPIRO**
   (12th Aug. 1961 – with
   You Don't Know)
14 **CILLA BLACK**
   (Feb. 22nd 1964 – with
   Anyone Who Had A Heart)

15 **SANDIE SHAW**
   (Oct. 31st 1964 – with
   **(There's) Always Something To
   Remind Me**)
16 **JACKIE TRENT**
   (May 22nd 1965 – with
   Where Are You Now?)
17 **NANCY SINATRA**
   (Feb. 19th 1966 – with
   **These Boots Are Made For
   Walkin'**)
18 **DUSTY SPRINGFIELD**
   (Apr. 23rd 1966 – with
   **You Don't Have To Say You Love
   Me**)
19 **PETULA CLARK**
   (Feb. 18th 1966 – with
   This Is My Song)
20 **MARY HOPKIN**
   (Oct. 5th 1968 – with
   Those Were The Days)

Despite the fact that Jo Stafford's 'You Belong To Me' was only the second single to top the newly-inaugurated British charts in 1953, this listing reveals that it took over 15 years for 19 further female solo artistes to equal Jo's feat. If nothing else, this suggests that there were many more girls during the 1950s and 60s buying records by male solo performers than vice versa!

Several of the ladies here topped the charts twice during the period covered by the listing, but surprisingly Sandie Shaw is the only one of the bunch to have managed it three times – with '(There's) Always Something There To Remind Me (1964), 'Long Live Love' (1965), and 'Puppet On A String' (1967).

THE FIRST TWENTY GIRL SINGERS TO TOP THE AMERICAN SINGLES CHART

Connie Francis

1 **DINAH SHORE**
(Oct. 5th 1944 – with
I'll Walk Alone)

2 **BETTY HUTTON**
(Feb. 21st 1946 – with
Doctor, Lawyer, Indian Chief)

3 **PEGGY LEE**
(Mar. 5th 1948 – with
Manana)

4 **MARGARET WHITING**
(Oct. 1st 1948 – with
A Tree In The Meadow)

5 **EVELYN KNIGHT**
(Jan. 14th 1949 – with
A Little Bird Told Me)

6 **TERESA BREWER**
(Mar. 10th 1950 – with
Mùsic! Music! Music!)

7 **EILEEN BARTON**
(Apr. 7th 1950 – with
**If I Knew You Were Comin' I'd've
Baked A Cake**)

8 **PATTI PAGE**
(Dec. 22nd 1950 – with
The Tennessee Waltz)

9 **ROSEMARY CLOONEY**
(Jul. 20th 1951 – with
Come On-A My House)

10 **KAY STARR**
(Mar. 7th 1952 – with
Wheel Of Fortune)

11 **VERA LYNN**
(Jul. 4th 1952 – with
Auf Weidersehen Sweetheart)

12 **JO STAFFORD**
(Sept. 5th 1952 – with
You Belong To Me)

13 **JONI JAMES**
(Nov. 22nd 1952 – with
Why Don't You Believe Me?)

14 **DORIS DAY**
(Feb. 17th 1954 – with
Secret Love)

15 **KITTY KALLEN**
(May 26th 1954 – with
Little Things Mean A Lot)

16 **JOAN WEBER**
(Jan. 12th 1955 – with
Let Me Go Lover)

17 **GOGI GRANT**
(Jun. 15th 1956 – with
The Wayward Wind)

18 **DEBBIE REYNOLDS**
(Aug. 30th 1957 – with
Tammy)

19 **CONNIE FRANCIS**
(Jun. 26th 1960 – with
Everybody's Somebody's Fool)

20 **BRENDA LEE**
(Jul. 17th 1960 – with
I'm Sorry)

It took sixteen years for America to have
twenty different girl chart-toppers (only
one of them – Vera Lynn – being a
non-American artist), but it should be
noted that several of these ladies,
including Patti Page, Kay Starr and
Rosemary Clooney, also went on to have
further chart-toppers after their initial
number one success.

THE FIRST TWENTY MILLION-SELLING SINGLES IN THE UK

Gary Glitter

1 **WHITE CHRISTMAS**
   Bing Crosby
   (released 1942)

2 **ROCK AROUND THE CLOCK**
   Bill Haley & The Comets
   (released 1954)

3 **MARY'S BOY CHILD**
   Harry Belafonte
   (released 1957)

4 **DIANA**
   Paul Anka
   (released 1957)

5 **IT'S NOW OR NEVER**
   Elvis Presley
   (released 1960)

6 **STRANGER ON THE SHORE**
   Mr Acker Bilk
   (released 1961)

7 **THE YOUNG ONES**
   Cliff Richard
   (released 1962)

8 **I REMEMBER YOU**
   Frank Ifield
   (released 1962)

9 **SHE LOVES YOU**
   Beatles
   (released 1963)

10 **I WANT TO HOLD YOUR HAND**
    Beatles
    (released 1963)

11 **CAN'T BUY ME LOVE**
    Beatles
    (released 1964)

12 **I FEEL FINE**
    Beatles
    (released 1964)

13 **TEARS**
    Ken Dodd
    (released 1965)

14 **THE CARNIVAL IS OVER**
    Seekers
    (released 1965)

15 **WE CAN WORK IT OUT**
    Beatles
    (released 1965)

16 **GREEN GREEN GRASS OF HOME**
    Tom Jones
    (released 1966)

17 **RELEASE ME**
    Engelbert Humperdinck
    (released 1967)

18 **THE LAST WALTZ**
    Engelbert Humperdinck
    (released 1967)

19 **EYE LEVEL**
    Simon Park Orchestra
    (released 1972)

20 **I LOVE YOU LOVE ME LOVE**
    Gary Glitter
    (released 1973)

Exactly when 'White Christmas' passed the million sales mark in Britain is hard to determine, partly because the earliest sales figures are hard to track down, and the British release rights changed hands from Decca to MCA along the way. Certainly by the time of Crosby's death in 1977, when the song became a top ten hit again, the huge sales boost had taken it well past seven figures. These twenty records are listed in the order of their release rather than the order in which they attained their million-seller status, for the selling periods involved vary considerably. Presley's 'It's Now Or Never' reached the target in six weeks, while the Beatles' 'I Want To Hold Your Hand', 'Can't Buy Me Love' and 'I Feel Fine' took only a matter of days. On the other hand, the Acker Bilk, Cliff Richard and Simon Park discs needed the best part of a decade to finally make the grade – although the bulk of their sales naturally came soon after their release.

THE FIRST TWENTY MILLION-SELLING SINGLES IN THE USA

1 **VESTI LA GIUBBA (ON WITH THE MOTLEY)**
Enrico Caruso
(released 1903)

2 **THE PREACHER AND THE BEAR**
Arthur Collins
(released 1905)

3 **RAGGING THE BABY TO SLEEP**
Al Jolson
(released 1912)

4 **THE SPANIARD THAT BLIGHTED MY LIFE**
Al Jolson
(released 1913)

5 **COHEN ON THE TELEPHONE**
Joe Hayman
(released 1914)

6 **CARRY ME BACK TO OLD VIRGINNY**
Alma Gluck
(released 1915)

7 **WANG DANG BLUES/HOT LIPS**
Henry Busse
(released 1920)

8 **DARDANELLA**
Ben Selvin
(released 1920)

9 **WHISPERING**
Paul Whiteman
(released 1920)

10 **WABASH BLUES**
Isham Jones
(released 1921)

11 **DREAMY MELODY**
Art Landry
(released 1922)

12 **THREE O'CLOCK IN THE MORNING**
Paul Whiteman
(released 1923)

13 **IT AIN'T GONNA RAIN NO MO'**
Wendell Hall
(released 1923)

14 **DOWN HEARTED BLUES**
Bessie Smith
(released 1923)

15 **SOMEBODY STOLE MY GAL**
Ted Weems
(released 1923)

16 **LINGER AWHILE**
Paul Whiteman
(released 1923)

17 **THE PRISONER'S SONG**
Vernon Dalhart
(released 1924)

18 **THE SINKING OF THE TITANIC**
Pop Stoneman
(released 1924)

19 **MY BLUE HEAVEN**
Gene Austin
(released 1927)

20 **IDA, SWEET AS APPLE CIDER**
Red Nichols & His Five Pennies
(released 1927)

Most of these recordings took several years to sell over a million copies, this era being the infancy of recording when the real music sales were still in the form of sheet music. Ironically, two of the first five records to reach seven-figure sales in the States were not wholly American; the opera tenor Enrico Caruso was born in Italy, and comedian Joe Hayman lived and worked (and recorded 'Cohen On The Telephone) in Britain, although he had been born in the USA.

The biggest sellers by far in this listing were 'Dardanella' by Ben Selvin – the first really big dance band disc – and Vernon Dalhart's 'The Prisoner's Song'. Both of these sold in excess of 6 million copies – a feat unmatched by all but the very biggest hits from later years.

THE FIRST TWENTY BEST-SELLER ALBUMS IN BRITAIN

1 **SOUTH PACIFIC**
Soundtrack
(released 1958)
2 **THE EXPLOSIVE FREDDY CANNON**
Freddy Cannon
(released 1960)
3 **ELVIS IS BACK**
Elvis Presley
(released 1960)
4 **DOWN DRURY LANE TO MEMORY LANE**
101 Strings
(released 1960)
5 **G.I. BLUES**
Elvis Presley
(released 1960)
6 **THE BLACK AND WHITE MINSTREL SHOW**
George Mitchell Minstrels
(released 1961)
7 **THE SHADOWS**
Shadows
(released 1961)
8 **21 TODAY**
Cliff Richard
(released 1961)
9 **ANOTHER BLACK AND WHITE MINSTREL SHOW**
George Mitchell Minstrels
(released 1961)
10 **BLUE HAWAII**
Elvis Presley
(released 1961)
11 **THE YOUNG ONES**
Cliff Richard
(released 1961)
12 **WEST SIDE STORY**
Soundtrack
(released 1962)
13 **POT LUCK**
Elvis Presley
(released 1962)
14 **A GOLDEN AGE OF DONEGAN**
Lonnie Donegan
(released 1962)

You've PLEASED PLEASED us!

Thank You, Folks

Paul
John
George
Ringo

15 **OUT OF THE SHADOWS**
Shadows
(released 1962)
16 **ON STAGE WITH THE MINSTRELS**
George Mitchell Minstrels
(released 1962)
17 **ELVIS: ROCK'N'ROLL NO. 2**
Elvis Presley
(released 1962)
18 **SUMMER HOLIDAY**
Cliff Richard
(released 1963)
19 **PLEASE PLEASE ME**
Beatles
(released 1963)
20 **WITH THE BEATLES**
Beatles
(released 1963)

Million-selling albums are few and far between in Britain; in fact, even today the BPI's Platinum Awards for albums are in recognition of one million pounds' worth of albums sold at factory-to-dealer price, which is in fact under half-a-million units. Large sales – as opposed to steady sales over long periods – were quite unknown in the UK until the advent of the Beatles, whose 'Please Please Me' album sold over 500,000, and 'With The Beatles' actually topped a million, the only LP to do so in the UK during the 60s.

THE FIRST TWENTY MILLION-SELLING ALBUMS IN THE USA

Glen Miller

1 **OKLAHOMA**
Original Stage Cast
(released 1949)

2 **SOUTH PACIFIC**
Original Stage Cast
(released 1949)

3 **AN AMERICAN IN PARIS**
Soundtrack
(released 1952)

4 **STRAUSS WALTZES**
Mantovani
(released 1953)

5 **CHRISTMAS CAROLS**
Mantovani
(released 1963)

6 **SONGS FROM 'THE STUDENT PRINCE' AND OTHERS**
Mario Lanza
(released 1954)

7 **THE GLENN MILLER STORY**
Glenn Miller
(released 1954)

8 **MANTOVANI PLAYS THE IMMORTAL CLASSICS**
Mantovani
(released 1954)

9 **MERRY CHRISTMAS**
Bing Crosby
(released 1954)

10 **RADIO BLOOPERS**
Kermit Schafer
(released 1954)

11 **OKLAHOMA**
Soundtrack
(released 1955)

12 **SONG HITS FROM THEATRELAND**
Mantovani
(released 1955)

13 **CALYPSO**
Harry Belafonte
(released 1956)

14 **MY FAIR LADY**
Original Stage Cast
(released 1956)

15 **HIGH SOCIETY**
Soundtrack
(released 1956)

16 **HYMNS**
Tennessee Ernie Ford
(released 1956)

17 **THE KING AND I**
Soundtrack
(released 1956)

18 **ELVIS PRESLEY**
Elvis Presley
(released 1956)

19 **FILM ENCORES**
Mantovani
(released 1957)

20 **ELVIS**
Elvis Presley
(released 1957)

Albums as we understand them – a 12-inch or 10-inch disc playing at 33⅓ rpm – first appeared in the USA in 1948. Prior to that, an album had meant a boxed-set collection of 78 rpm singles, and both the 'Oklahoma' stage cast music and Bing Crosby's 'Merry Christmas' set had earlier appeared in this form.

It can be easily seen that show, screen and light orchestral music hogged the really big sales in the early album years, with Kermit Schafer's 'Radio Bloopers' comedy set providing rousing relief. The two Presley albums at the very end of the list were the first two really youth-oriented LPs to sell in huge quantities.

THE FIRST TWENTY MILLION-SELLING ALBUMS BY ROCK ARTISTS (WORLDWIDE)

1 **ELVIS PRESLEY**
Elvis Presley
(released 1956)

2 **ELVIS**
Elvis Presley
(released 1957)

3 **ELVIS' CHRISTMAS ALBUM**
Elvis Presley
(released 1957)

4 **ELVIS' GOLDEN RECORDS**
Elvis Presley
(released 1958)

5 **THE BUDDY HOLLY STORY**
Buddy Holly
(released 1959)

6 **50,000,000 ELVIS FANS CAN'T BE WRONG (GOLDEN RECORDS VOL. 2)**
Elvis Presley
(released 1960)

7 **G.I. BLUES**
Elvis Presley
(released 1960)

8 **BLUE HAWAII**
Elvis Presley
(released 1961)

9 **MODERN SOUNDS IN COUNTRY AND WESTERN MUSIC**
Ray Charles
(released 1962)

10 **PETER, PAUL AND MARY**
Peter, Paul And Mary
(released 1962)

11 **GIRLS! GIRLS! GIRLS!**
Elvis Presley
(released 1963)

12 **WITH THE BEATLES**
Beatles*
(released 1963)

13 **MEET THE BEATLES**
Beatles*
(released 1964)

14 **INTRODUCING THE BEATLES**
Beatles
(released 1964)

15 **A HARD DAY'S NIGHT**
Beatles
(released 1964)

16 **SOMETHING NEW**
Beatles
(released 1964)

17 **BEATLES FOR SALE**
Beatles**
(released 1964)

18 **BEATLES '65**
Beatles**
(released 1964)

19 **THE BEATLES' STORY**
Beatles
(released 1964)

20 **BEATLES IV**
Beatles
(released 1965)

A case of total domination by the two names you would most expect to see there. Across the rock world in general, albums remained very much the minor interest alongside hit singles until the progressive rock explosion and the emergence of album-oriented artists like Bob Dylan in the mid-60s. Presley and the Beatles were the exceptions to the general rule simply because their supergiant stature meant they had almost as many fans wanting to buy their albums as brought their million-selling singles.

The two Beatles albums marked * and the two marked ** were the substantially different American and British versions of a similar release. Since in each case both versions sold a million (on different sides of the Atlantic), they are listed here separately.

THE FIRST TWENTY MILLION-SELLING ALBUMS BY AMERICAN ROCK ARTISTS OTHER THAN ELVIS PRESLEY

Buddy Holly

1 **THE BUDDY HOLLY STORY**
   Buddy Holly
   (released 1959)

2 **MODERN SOUNDS IN COUNTRY AND WESTERN MUSIC**
   Ray Charles
   (released 1962)

3 **PETER, PAUL AND MARY**
   Peter, Paul And Mary
   (released 1962)

4 **LOOK AT US**
   Sonny And Cher
   (released 1965)

5 **HIGHWAY 61 REVISITED**
   Bob Dylan
   (released 1965)

6 **IF YOU CAN BELIEVE YOUR EYES AND EARS**
   Mamas & The Papas
   (released 1966)

7 **THE MONKEES**
   Monkees
   (released 1966)

8 **THE MAMAS AND THE PAPAS**
   Mamas & The Papas
   (released 1966)

9 **MORE OF THE MONKEES**
   Monkees
   (released 1967)

10 **THE DOORS**
   Doors
   (released 1967)

11 **HEADQUARTERS**
   Monkees
   (released 1967)

12 **GREATEST HITS**
   Diana Ross & The Supremes
   (released 1967)

13 **PISCES , AQUARIUS, CAPRICORN AND JONES LTD.**
   Monkees
   (released 1967)

14 **IN-A-GADDA-DA-VIDA**
   Iron Butterfly
   (released 1968)

15 **T.C.B.**
   Diana Ross & The Supremes with The Temptations
   (released 1968)

16 **BLOOD, SWEAT & TEARS**
   Blood, Sweat & Tears
   (released 1968)

17 **BAYOU COUNTRY**
   Creedence Clearwater Revival
   (released 1969)

18 **CROSBY, STILLS AND NASH**
   Crosby, Stills and Nash
   (released 1969)

19 **THE AGE OF AQUARIUS**
   5th Dimension
   (released 1969)

20 **SANTANA**
   Santana
   (released 1969)

As already shown elsewhere, pop/rock album sales in seven figures were extremely rare through the fifties and early sixties, but by the middle of the latter decade, the very hottest acts were starting to sell as many albums as they did singles (as in the case of the Mamas & Papas and the Monkees), and in the latter sixties the situation began to arise where the album was an act's focal point (Blood, Sweat & Tears, Iron Butterfly, Santana, CS&N) and hit singles might be extracted from it as bonus sellers. This very much set the stage for the album-dominated rock world of the seventies.

THE FIRST TWENTY MILLION-SELLING ALBUMS BY BRITISH ROCK ARTISTS OTHER THAN THE BEATLES

The Rolling Stones

1 **OUT OF OUR HEADS**
Rolling Stones
(released 1965)

2 **THE BEST OF HERMAN'S HERMITS**
Herman's Hermits
(released 1965)

3 **DECEMBER'S CHILDREN (AND EVERYBODY'S)**
Rolling Stones
(released 1965)

4 **THE BEST OF THE ANIMALS**
Animals
(released 1966)

5 **AFTERMATH**
Rolling Stones
(released 1966)

6 **BIG HITS (HIGH TIDE AND GREEN GRASS)**
Rolling Stones
(released 1966)

7 **DISRAELI GEARS**
Cream
(released 1967)

8 **DAYS OF FUTURE PASSED**
Moody Blues
(released 1967)

9 **THEIR SATANIC MAJESTIES REQUEST**
Rolling Stones
(released 1967)

10 **FEVER ZONE**
Tom Jones
(released 1968)

11 **WHEELS OF FIRE**
Cream
(released 1968)

12 **THIS IS TOM JONES**
Tom Jones
(released 1969)

13 **LED ZEPPELIN**
Led Zeppelin
(released 1969)

14 **THROUGH THE PAST, DARKLY (BIG HITS VOL. 2)**
Rolling Stones
(released 1969)

15 **LED ZEPPELIN II**
Led Zeppelin
(released 1969)

16 **TOMMY**
The Who
(released 1969)

17 **LIVE IN LAS VEGAS**
Tom Jones
(released 1969)

18 **LET IT BLEED**
Rolling Stones
(released 1969)

19 **LED ZEPPELIN III**
Led Zeppelin
(released 1970)

20 **A QUESTION OF BALANCE**
Moody Blues
(released 1970)

This listing is based upon worldwide sales estimates, although in every case the lion's share of the sales came from the USA. The growth of albums as a rock medium became more and more pronounced as the 1960s drew to an end, as witness the large number of British artists who achieved million-selling albums during 1969. Several of the acts here, notably the Rolling Stones (who dominate this list), the Moody Blues and Led Zeppelin, continue to make million-selling hit albums into the 1980s.

THE FIRST TWENTY MILLION-SELLING ROCK'N'ROLL SINGLES IN THE USA

Frankie Lymon & The Teenagers

1 ROCK AROUND THE CLOCK
   Bill Haley & The Comets
   (released 1954 – reached 1)

2 SHAKE, RATTLE AND ROLL
   Bill Haley & The Comets
   (released 1954 – reached 7)

3 MAYBELLINE
   Chuck Berry
   (released 1955 – reached 5)

4 AIN'T THAT A SHAME
   Fats Domino
   (released 1955 – reached 16)

5 AIN'T THAT A SHAME
   Pat Boone
   (released 1955 – reached 2)

6 SEVENTEEN
   Boyd Bennett
   (released 1955 – reached 5)

7 I HEAR YOU KNOCKING
   Gale Storm
   (released 1955 – reached 2)

8 SEE YOU LATER ALLIGATOR
   Bill Haley & The Comets
   (released 1955 – reached 6)

9 TUTTI FRUTTI
   Little Richard
   (released 1955 – reached 15)

10 HEARTBREAK HOTEL
   Elvis Presley
   (released 1956 – reached 1)

11 BLUE SUEDE SHOES
   Carl Perkins
   (released 1956 – reached 4)

12 I'M IN LOVE AGAIN
   Fats Domino
   (released 1956 – reached 5)

13 WHY DO FOOLS FALL IN LOVE?
   Teenagers featuring Frankie Lymon
   (released 1956 – reached 7)

14 I WANT YOU, I NEED YOU, I LOVE YOU
   Elvis Presley
   (released 1956 – reached 3)

15 LONG TALL SALLY
   Little Richard
   (released 1956 – reached 13)

16 BLUEBERRY HILL
   Fats Domino
   (released 1956 – reached 4)

17 BE-BOP-A-LULA
   Gene Vincent
   (released 1956 – reached 9)

18 HOUND DOG
   Elvis Presley
   (released 1956 – reached 2)

19 DON'T BE CRUEL
   Elvis Presley
   (released 1956 – reached 1)

20 HONKY TONK (PART 2)
   Bill Doggett
   (released 1956 – reached 2)

As rock'n'roll came to be a recognisable musical genre in its own right, growing from a hybrid of R&B and Country Rockabilly it was at first a little hard to draw distinctions between the various kinds of music. By the mid-50s, however, the rock bandwagon was rolling, and these were the first twenty million-selling singles which clearly belong in that category.

THE FIRST TWENTY MILLION-SELLING SINGLES OF THE 1970s

1 RAINDROPS KEEP FALLIN'
   ON MY HEAD
   B. J. Thomas

2 WHOLE LOTTA LOVE
   Led Zeppelin

3 I WANT YOU BACK
   Jackson 5

4 VENUS
   Shocking Blue

5 JAM UP JELLY TIGHT
   Tommy Roe

6 DON'T CRY DADDY
   Elvis Presley

7 THANK YOU (FALLETINME BE
   MICE ELF AGIN)
   Sly & The Family Stone

8 WITHOUT LOVE
   Tom Jones

9 BRIDGE OVER TROUBLED
   WATER
   Simon and Garfunkel

10 HEY THERE LONELY GIRL
   Eddie Holman

11 NO TIME
   Guess Who

12 TRAVELLIN' BAND
   Creedence Clearwater Revival

13 RAINY NIGHT IN GEORGIA
   Brook Benton

14 THE RAPPER
   Jaggerz

15 MA BELLE AMIE
   Tee-Set

16 LET IT BE
   Beatles

17 ABC
   Jackson 5

18 LOVE GROWS
   Edison Lighthouse

19 INSTANT KARMA
   **John Ono Lennon
   & The Plastic Ono Band**

20 SPIRIT IN THE SKY
   Norman Greenbaum

The seventies got underway with a slew of classic million-selling hit singles and several one-offs; the hits by the Jaggerz, Norman Greenbaum, Edison Lighthouse and the Dutch group Tee-Set falling into the latter category. 'Let It Be' marked the virtual end of the Beatles and the close of an era, but Led Zeppelin's 'Whole Lotta Love' (which sold a million in the USA but was never issued as a single in Britain) and the Jackson 5's two million-sellers were to mark the start of a decade of chart prosperity for these two groups. Just two of the artists here – Elvis Presley and Brook Benton – had been making million sellers (or any kind of hits) ten years earlier at the start of the sixties.

THE FIRST TWENTY MILLION-SELLING R&B/SOUL SINGLES OF THE 60s

Ray Charles

1 **FINGER POPPIN' TIME**
Hank Ballard & The Midnighters
(released 1960)

2 **NIGHT**
Jackie Wilson
(released 1960)

3 **BABY (YOU GOT WHAT IT TAKES)**
Brook Benton &
Dinah Washington
(released 1960)

4 **WALKIN' TO NEW ORLEANS**
Fats Domino
(released 1960)

5 **LET'S GO, LET'S GO, LET'S GO**
Hank Ballard & The Midnighters
(released 1960)

6 **KIDDIO**
Brook Benton
(released 1960)

7 **GEORGIA ON MY MIND**
Ray Charles
(released 1960)

8 **CHAIN GANG**
Sam Cooke
(released 1960)

9 **I LOVE THE WAY YOU LOVE**
Marv Johnson
(released 1960)

10 **SAVE THE LAST DANCE FOR ME**
Drifters
(released 1960)

11 **STAY**
Maurice Williams & The Zodiacs
(released 1960)

12 **ONE MINT JULEP**
Ray Charles
(released 1961)

13 **SHOP AROUND**
Miracles
(released 1960)

14 **TOSSIN' AND TURNIN'**
Bobby Lewis
(released 1961)

15 **THE BOLL WEEVIL SONG**
Brook Benton
(released 1961)

16 **RAINDROPS**
Dee Clark
(released 1961)

17 **ONE HUNDRED POUNDS OF**
CLAY
Gene McDaniels
(released 1961)

18 **HIT THE ROAD, JACK**
Ray Charles
(released 1961)

19 **EVERY BEAT OF MY HEART**
Pips
(released 1961)

20 **I LIKE IT LIKE THAT**
Chris Kenner
(released 1961)

Rhythm and Blues, which had jointly (with Country Rockabilly) given birth to rock'n'roll, during the 1950s' became almost inextricably tied up with it for most of the remainder of that decade. As the excitement of white rock began to mellow into teenbeat, however, R&B began to take its own path again, thanks to several artists with strong and distinctive styles who were to help mould it into the soul music of the next decade. The major names amongst these – Ray Charles, Sam Cooke and Jackie Wilson, plus the Drifters vocal group – are prominent in this listing of early 60s million sellers.

THE FIRST TWENTY 'BRITISH INVASION' MILLION SELLERS IN THE USA

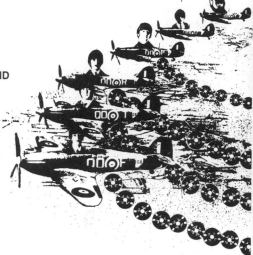

1 I WANT TO HOLD YOUR HAND
   Beatles
   (released 1964 – reached 1)

2 SHE LOVES YOU
   Beatles
   (released 1964 – reached 1)

3 PLEASE PLEASE ME
   Beatles
   (released 1963 – reached 3)

4 TWIST AND SHOUT
   Beatles
   (released 1964 – reached 1)

5 GLAD ALL OVER
   Dave Clark Five
   (released 1964 – reached 5)

6 CAN'T BUY ME LOVE
   Beatles
   (released 1964 – reached 1)

7 NEEDLES AND PINS
   Searchers
   (released 1964 – reached 12)

8 DO YOU WANT TO KNOW A SECRET?
   Beatles
   (released 1964 – reached 2)

9 BITS AND PIECES
   Dave Clark Five
   (released 1964 – reached 4)

10 LOVE ME DO
   Beatles
   (released 1964 – reached 1)

11 LITTLE CHILDREN/BAD TO ME
   Billy J Kramer & The Dakotas
   (released 1964 – reached 7 & 9)

12 WORLD WITHOUT LOVE
   Peter & Gordon
   (released 1964 – reached 1)

13 MY BOY LOLLIPOP
   Millie
   (released 1964 – reached 3)

14 DON'T LET THE SUN CATCH YOU CRYING
   Gerry & The Pacemakers
   (released 1964 – reached 4)

15 CAN'T YOU SEE THAT SHE'S MINE?
   Dave Clark Five
   (released 1964 – reached 4)

16 A HARD DAY'S NIGHT
   Beatles
   (released 1964 – reached 1)

17 WISHIN' AND HOPIN'
   Dusty Springfield
   (released 1964 – reached 5)

18 BECAUSE
   Dave Clark Five
   (released 1964 – reached 4)

19 THE HOUSE OF THE RISING SUN
   Animals
   (released 1964 – reached 1)

20 DO WAH DIDDY DIDDY
   Manfred Mann
   (released 1964 – reached 1)

It's a quite staggering fact that between February and October 1964, twenty British singles, by eight different groups and two girl soloists, sold a million copies in the USA – the previously – 'unconquerable' market. That is why Americans have always referred to it as 'The British Invasion'.

THE FIRST TEN MILLION-SELLING COMEDY ALBUMS

1 **RADIO BLOOPERS**
   Kermit Schafer
   (released 1953)

2 **SONGS FOR SINNERS**
   Rusty Warren
   (released 1958)

3 **KNOCKERS UP**
   Rusty Warren
   (released 1959)

4 **IF I EMBARRASS YOU,
   TELL YOUR FRIENDS**
   Belle Barth
   (released 1960)

5 **THE FIRST FAMILY**
   Vaughn Meader
   (released 1962)

6 **MY SON, THE FOLK SINGER**
   Allan Sherman
   (released 1962)

7 **BILL COSBY IS A VERY
   FUNNY FELLOW, RIGHT?**
   Bill Cosby
   (released 1964)

8 **I STARTED OUT AS A CHILD**
   Bill Cosby
   (released 1964)

9 **WELCOME TO THE LBJ RANCH**
   Earle Doud & Allen Robin
   (released 1965)

10 **WHY IS THERE AIR?**
    Bill Cosby
    (released 1965)

Million-selling albums of comedy rather than music have been fairly rare through the years. Most of those listed above were one-off successes selling on their novelty value: notably the spoofs on presidential families by Vaughn Meader and Robin & Doud. The Rusty Warren and Belle Barth albums were bluish adult comedy which sold from word-of-mouth promotion without any airplay. Clearly, Bill Cosby was king of the comedy sellers, though, with three albums in the listing above and a fourth million-seller, 'Wonderfulness', in 1966.

THE FIRST TWENTY MILLION-SELLING COUNTRY MUSIC SINGLES IN THE USA

The Carter Family

1 **THE PRISONER'S SONG**
   Vernon Dalhart
   (released 1924)

2 **THE SINKING OF THE TITANIC**
   Pop Stoneman
   (released 1924)

3 **WILDWOOD FLOWER**
   Carter Family
   (released 1928)

4 **BLUE YODEL**
   Jimmie Rodgers
   (released 1928)

5 **BRAKEMAN'S BLUES**
   Jimmie Rodgers
   (released 1928)

6 **DOWN YONDER**
   Gid Tanner
   (released 1934)

7 **THAT SILVER-HAIRED DADDY OF MINE**
   Gene Autry
   (released 1939)

8 **WALKIN' THE FLOOR OVER YOU**
   Ernest Tubb
   (released 1941)

9 **WHEN MY BLUE MOON TURNS TO GOLD AGAIN**
   Wiley Walker & Gene Sullivan
   (released 1941)

10 **WABASH CANNONBALL**
    Roy Acuff
    (released 1942)

11 **THERE'S A STAR-SPANGLED BANNER WAVING SOMEWHERE**
    Elton Britt
    (released 1942)

12 **BORN TO LOSE**
    Ted Daffan & The Texans
    (released 1943)

13 **PISTOL PACKIN' MAMA**
    Al Dexter & His Troopers
    (released 1943)

14 **GUITAR BOOGIE**
    Arthur Smith
    (released 1945)

15 **I'LL HOLD YOU IN MY HEART**
    Eddy Arnold
    (released 1947)

16 **HERE COMES SANTA CLAUS**
    Gene Autry
    (released 1947)

17 **NEW JOLE BLON**
    Moon Mullican
    (released 1947)

18 **SMOKE, SMOKE, SMOKE THAT CIGARETTE**
    Tex Williams
    (released 1947)

19 **BOUQUET OF ROSES/ TEXARKANA BABY**
    Eddy Arnold
    (released 1948)

20 **TENNESSEE WALTZ**
    Cowboy Copas
    (released 1948)

Strange but true – before the 50s had even dawned, before the era of Hank Williams and then the growth of the 'Nashville' sound, more than twenty records by Country Music (originally hillbilly) artists had sold a million copies. Some of these names look very esoteric to modern eyes, but they were all big stars in their day. Artists like Eddy Arnold and Roy Acuff, however, continued to sell records for many years afterwards (Arnold up to the present day), and these – along with Gene Autry for his many film appearances – are better remembered.

THE FIRST TEN MILLION-SELLING COUNTRY MUSIC ALBUMS

Tammy Wynette

Johnny Cash

1 **HYMNS**
   Tennessee Ernie Ford
   (released 1956)

2 **MODERN SOUNDS IN COUNTRY AND WESTERN MUSIC**
   Ray Charles
   (released 1962)

3 **GREATEST HITS**
   Johnny Cash
   (released 1967)

4 **JOHNNY CASH AT FOLSOM PRISON**
   Johnny Cash
   (released 1968)

5 **HARPER VALLEY P.T.A.**
   Jeannie C Riley
   (released 1968)

6 **GLEN CAMPBELL LIVE**
   Glen Campbell
   (released 1969)

7 **JOHNNY CASH AT SAN QUENTIN**
   Johnny Cash
   (released 1969)

8 **TAMMY WYNETTE'S GREATEST HITS**
   Tammy Wynette
   (released 1969)

9 **THE BEST OF CHARLEY PRIDE**
   Charley Pride
   (released 1969)

10 **HELLO I'M JOHNNY CASH**
   Johnny Cash
   (released 1970)

Nat 'King' Cole's 'Ramblin' Rose' album, featuring entirely country songs, was also a million seller in 1962/3. A further package, titled 'Famous Original Hits' and featuring 25 country classics sung by the original artists, also sold over a million copies in 1965. It was compiled by the Country Music Association in aid of the establishment of the CMA Museum in Nashville, and was sold only by mail order, thus never featuring on any LP sales chart.

ELVIS PRESLEY'S FIRST TEN SINGLES (USA RELEASES)

THAT'S ALL RIGHT MAMA/
Blue Moon Of Kentucky
Sun 209 (Jul. 1954)

GOOD ROCKIN' TONIGHT/
I Don't Care If The Sun Don't Shine
Sun 210 (Sept. 1954)

YOU'RE A HEARTBREAKER/
Milk Cow Blues Boogie
Sun 215 (Jan. 1955)

BABY LET'S PLAY HOUSE/
I'm Left, You're Right, She's Gone
Sun 217 (Apr. 1955)

I FORGOT TO REMEMBER TO
FORGET/Mystery Train
Sun 223 (Aug. 1955)

HEARTBREAK HOTEL/
I Was The One
RCA 6420 (Feb. 1956)

I WANT YOU, I NEED YOU, I
LOVE YOU/My Baby Left Me
RCA 6540 (May 1956)

HOUND DOG/DON'T BE CRUEL
RCA 6604 (Jul. 1954)

LOVE ME TENDER/
Any Way You Want Me
RCA 6643 (Oct. 1956)

TOO MUCH/Playing For Keeps
RCA 6800 (Jan. 1957)

Sun Records was the small independent label in Memphis, Tennessee where Elvis Presley's recording career – and effectively, the rock'n'roll revolution – was born. The first of the Sun releases to find national success was 'I Forgot To Remember To Forget', which made the top ten in the Country & Western charts. When Elvis moved to RCA, he promptly sold over a million of the next five singles – several million in the case of the double A-side 'Hound Dog'/'Don't Be Cruel'. RCA also reissued the Sun singles with new catalogue numbers when they bought his contract, but these have been ignored for the purposes of this listing – . as has the batch of discs which were all issued on the same day to offer buyers the contents of this first album in singles form.

ELVIS PRESLEY'S FIRST TEN ALBUMS (USA RELEASES)

ELVIS PRESLEY
LPM 1254

ELVIS
LPM 1382

LOVING YOU (film soundtrack)
LPM 1515

ELVIS' CHRISTMAS ALBUM
LOC 1035

ELVIS' GOLDEN RECORDS
LPM 1701

KING CREOLE (film soundtrack)
LPM 1884

FOR LP FANS ONLY
LPM 1990

A DATE WITH ELVIS
LPM 2011

50,000,000 ELVIS FANS CAN'T BE
WRONG: ELVIS' GOLDEN RECORDS
VOL. 2
LPM 2075

ELVIS IS BACK
LPM 2231 mono/LSP 2231 stereo

As documented elsewhere in this book, many of these albums were million-sellers, including those which were compilations of previously million-selling singles! 'Elvis Is Back', recorded after he came out of the army, was Presley's first release to be made and released in stereo.

THE BEATLES' FIRST TEN SINGLES (UK RELEASES)

MY BONNIE/The Saints
Polydor NH 66-833
Credited to Tony Sheridan and The
Beatles (Jan. 1962)

LOVE ME DO/ P.S. I Love You
Parlophone R 4949 (Oct. 1962)

PLEASE PLEASE ME/Ask Me Why
Parlophone R 4983 (Jan. 1963)

FROM ME TO YOU/Thank You Girl
Parlophone R 5015 (Apr. 1963)

SHE LOVES YOU/I'll Get You
Parlophone R 5055 (Aug. 1963)

**I WANT TO HOLD YOUR HAND/
This Boy**
Parlophone R 5084 (Nov. 1963)

WHY/Cry For A Shadow
Polydor NH 52-275 (Feb. 1964)

**CAN'T BUY ME LOVE/
You Can't Do That**
Parlophone R 5114 (Mar. 1964)

**AIN'T SHE SWEET/
If You Love Me Baby**
Polydor NH 52-317 (May 1964)

**A HARD DAY'S NIGHT/
Things We Said Today**
Parlophone R 5160 (Jul. 1964)

Not a lot to say about these, except to
note the obvious fact that the three
Polydor singles come from the Beatles
pre-Parlophone Hamburg sessions with
Bert Kaempfert, when they were the
backup group for Tony Sheridan. The
two tracks 'Cry For A Shadow' and 'Ain't
She Sweet' on these singles are by the
Beatles without Sheridan; the former is
an instrumental (their attempt to "do
something like the Shadows' 'Apache' " –
hence the title!), while the latter has John
Lennon on lead vocal.

THE BEATLES' FIRST TEN ALBUMS (UK RELEASES)

PLEASE PLEASE ME
PCS 3042 (1963)

WITH THE BEATLES
PCS 3045 (1963)

THE BEATLES' FIRST
Polydor 236-201 (1964)

A HARD DAY'S NIGHT
PCS 3058 (1964)

BEATLES FOR SALE
PCS 3062 (1964)

HELP!
PCS 3071 (1965)

RUBBER SOUL
PCS 3075 (1965)

REVOLVER
PCS 7009 (1966)

**A COLLECTION OF BEATLES OLDIES
(BUT GOLDIES)**
PCS 7016 (1966)

**SERGEANT PEPPER'S LONELY
HEARTS CLUB BAND**
PCS 7027 (1967)

Apart from 'The Beatles' First' (a
compilation of all their German Polydor
tracks), and 'A Collection . . .', all these
were massive-selling number one
albums, which still sell today.

THE ROLLING STONES' FIRST TEN SINGLES (UK RELEASES)

COME ON/I Want To Be Loved
Decca F 11675 (Jun. 1963)

I WANNA BE YOUR MAN/Stoned
Decca F 11764 (Nov. 1963)

NOT FADE AWAY/Little By Little
Decca F 11845 (Feb. 1964)

IT'S ALL OVER NOW/
Good Times, Bad Times
Decca F 11934 (Jun. 1964))

LITTLE RED ROOSTER/Off The Hook
Decca F 12014 (Nov. 1964)

THE LAST TIME/Play With Fire
Decca F 12104 (Feb. 1965)

(I CAN'T GET NO) SATISFACTION/
The Spider And The Fly
Decca F 12220 (Aug. 1965)

GET OFF OF MY CLOUD/
The Singer Not The Song
Decca F 12263 (Oct. 1965)

19th NERVOUS BREAKDOWN/
As Tears Go By
Decca F 12331 (Feb. 1966)

PAINT IT BLACK/Long Long While
Decca F 12395 (May 1966)

The Stones' first five A-sides were all cover versions (of Chuck Berry, the Beatles, Buddy Holly, the Valentinos and Sam Cooke), but from 'The Last Time' onwards, their hits were all Jagger/Richard compositions. 'Come On' was the only one of these singles not to reach the top ten in Britain, while all the singles here from 'Little Red Rooster' onwards were number one hits.

THE ROLLING STONES' FIRST TEN ALBUMS (UK RELEASES)

THE ROLLING STONES
DECCA   LK 4605 (1964)
THE ROLLING STONES NO. 2
DECCA   SKL 4661 (1965)
OUT OF OUR HEADS
DECCA   SKL 4733 (1965)
AFTERMATH
DECCA   SKL 4786 (1966)
BIG HITS (HIGH TIDE AND GREEN GRASS)
DECCA   TXS 101 (1966)
BETWEEN THE BUTTONS
DECCA   SKL 4852 (1967)
THEIR SATANIC MAJESTIES REQUEST
DECCA   TXS 103 (1967)
BEGGARS BANQUET
DECCA   SKL 4955 (1968)
THROUGH THE PAST, DARKLY (BIG HITS VOL. 2)
DECCA   SKL 5019 (1969)
LET IT BLEED
DECCA   SKL 5025 (1969)

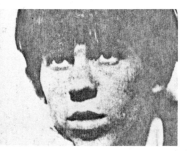

This album release pattern differed considerably from that followed in the States, with similarly titled sets having substantially different track line-ups. By making use of singles cuts and some extra material, not released in Britain at the times, the group's US label was also able to come up with additional releases like '12x5', 'December's Children (And Everybody's)', 'Got LIVE If You Want It', and 'Flowers'.

The who

MAXIMUM R&B

TUESDAYS AT THE MARQUEE
90 WARDOUR ST

THE WHO'S FIRST TEN SINGLES (UK RELEASES)

I'M THE FACE/Zoot Suit
Fontana TF 480 (1964)

I CAN'T EXPLAIN/Bald Headed Woman
Brunswick 05926 (Feb. 1965)

ANYWAY ANYHOW ANYWHERE/Daddy Rolling Stone
Brunswick 05935 (May 1965)

MY GENERATION/Shout And Shimmy
Brunswick 05944 (Oct. 1965)

SUBSTITUTE/Circles
Reaction 591001 (Mar. 1966)

SUBSTITUTE/Waltz For A Pig
Reaction 591001 (Mar. 1966)

A LEGAL MATTER/Instant Party
Brunswick 05956 (Mar. 1966)

THE KIDS ARE ALRIGHT/The Ox
Brunswick 05965 (Aug. 1966)

I'M A BOY/In The City
Reaction 591004 (Aug. 1966)

LA-LA-LA-LIES/The Good's Gone
Brunswick 05968 (Oct. 1966)

The first single, 'I'm The Face', was issued under the group's previous name of the High Numbers; it failed to sell and became a valuable collectors' item in later years. 'Substitute' was released twice with different flip-sides because of legal complications over the track 'Circles' (which is in fact identical to 'Instant Party' on the B-side of 'A Legal Matter'). 'Waltz For A Pig', which replaced it, is not by the Who at all, but is credited to 'The Who Orchestra', in reality the Graham Bond Organisation. Brunswick singles after 'Substitute' were made up of tracks from the group's first album, issued to compete with subsequent Reaction singles.

THE WHO'S FIRST TEN ALBUMS (UK RELEASES)

MY GENERATION
Brunswick LAT 8616 (1965)

A QUICK ONE
Reaction 593002 (1966)

THE WHO SELL OUT
Track 613002 (1967)

DIRECT HITS
Track 613006 (1969)

TOMMY
Track 613013/613014 –
double LP (1969)

LIVE AT LEEDS
Track 2406 001 (1970)

MEATY, BEATY, BIG AND BOUNCY
Track 2406 006 (1971)

WHO'S NEXT
Track 2408 102 (1971)

QUADROPHENIA
Track 2657 013 (1973)

ODDS AND SODS
Track 2406 116 (1974)

'Direct Hits', 'Meaty, Beaty, Big & Bouncy' and 'Odds And Sods' were all compilations of singles cuts or unissued material. During the period of this listing, Pete Townshend of the Who also had a solo album, 'Who Came First'. It was released in 1972 On Track 2408 210.

CLIFF RICHARD'S FIRST TEN SINGLES (UK RELEASES)

MOVE IT/Schoolboy Crush
Columbia DB 4178 (Aug. 1958)

HIGH CLASS BABY/
My Feet Hit The Ground
Columbia DB 4203 (Nov. 1958)

LIVIN' LOVIN' DOLL/Steady With You
Columbia DB 4249 (Jan. 1959)

MEAN STREAK/Never Mind
Columbia DB 4290 (Apr. 1959)

LIVING DOLL/Apron Strings
Columbia DB 4306 (Jul. 1959)

TRAVELLIN' LIGHT/Dynamite
Columbia DB 4351 (Oct. 1959)

A VOICE IN THE WILDERNESS/
Don't Be Mad At Me
Columbia DB 4398 (Jan. 1960)

FALL IN LOVE WITH YOU/
Willie And The Hand Jive
Columbia DB 4431 (Mar. 1960)

PLEASE DON'T TEASE/
Where Is My Heart?
Columbia DB 4479 (Jun. 1960)

NINE TIMES OUT OF TEN/
Thinking Of Our Love
Columbia DB 4506 (Sept. 1960)

'Move It' was initially released as the B-side of 'Schoolboy Crush', but soon asserted its superiority and took Cliff to a debut placing of number 2 in the UK charts. Following that, every release here except 'Livin' Lovin' Doll' reached the top 5, while 'Living Doll', 'Travellin' Light' and 'Please Don't Tease' were all chart-toppers. Cliff's flipsides 'Never Mind', 'Dynamite' and 'Willie And The Hand Jive' also charted in the top 30 in their own right.

CLIFF RICHARD'S FIRST TEN ALBUMS (UK RELEASES)

CLIFF
COLUMBIA SX 1147 (1959)

CLIFF SINGS
COLUMBIA SX 1192 (1959)

ME AND MY SHADOWS
COLUMBIA SX 1261 (1960)

LISTEN TO CLIFF
COLUMBIA SX 1320 (1961)

21 TODAY
COLUMBIA SX 1368 (1961)

THE YOUNG ONES
COLUMBIA SX 1384 (1962)

32 MINUTES AND 17 SECONDS
WITH CLIFF RICHARD
COLUMBIA SX 1431 (1962)

SUMMER HOLIDAY
COLUMBIA SX 1472 (1963)

CLIFF'S HIT ALBUM
COLUMBIA SX 1512 (1963)

WHEN IN SPAIN
COLUMBIA SX 1541 (1963)

Cliff also had six tracks on the 1959 album of Jack Good's 'Oh Boy' TV show, which featured an assortment of rock artists. This was issued on Parlophone PMC 1072. Of the albums above, 'Cliff's Hit Album' was a compilation of singles A-sides from 1958-62, while 'The Young Ones' and 'Summer Holiday' were the soundtracks to his first two starring musical films, and also featured tracks by the Shadows and various cast members.

CHUCK BERRY'S FIRST TEN SINGLES (USA RELEASES)

MAYBELLINE/Wee Wee Hours
Chess 1604 (Jun. 1955)

THIRTY DAYS/
Together (We Will Always Be)
Chess 1615 (Oct. 1955)

NO MONEY DOWN/Downbound Train
Chess 1610 (Jan. 1956)

ROLL OVER BEETHOVEN/
Drifting Heart
Chess 1626 (May 1956)

BROWN-EYED HANDSOME MAN/
Too Much Monkey Business
Chess 1635 (Sept. 1956)

YOU CAN'T CATCH ME/Havana Moon
Chess 1645 (Dec. 1956)

SCHOOL DAY/Deep Feeling
Chess 1653 (Mar. 1957)

OH BABY DOLL/La Juanda (Espanol)
Chess 1664 (Jul. 1957)

ROCK AND ROLL MUSIC/Blue Feeling
Chess 1671 (Oct. 1957)

SWEET LITTLE SIXTEEN/
Reelin' And Rockin'
Chess 1683 (Jan. 1958)

Chuck Berry was one of rock and roll's most influential songwriters and certainly its most influential guitarist. From the early 1960's onwards, artists and groups have been playing and recording these songs continuously with many of the titles above being recognisable even to the casual observer as rock standards.

CHUCK BERRY'S FIRST TEN ALBUMS (USA RELEASES)

AFTER SCHOOL SESSION
CHESS 1426 (1958)

ONE DOZEN BERRIES
CHESS 1432 (1958)

CHUCK BERRY IS ON TOP
CHESS 1435 (1959)

ROCKIN' AT THE HOPS
CHESS 1448 (1960)

NEW JUKE BOX HITS
CHESS 1456 (1961)

MORE CHUCK BERRY
CHESS 1465 (1962)

CHUCK BERRY ON STAGE
CHESS 1480 (1963)

CHUCK BERRY'S GREATEST HITS
CHESS 1485 (1964)

ST. LOUIS TO LIVERPOOL
CHESS 1488 (1964)

CHUCK BERRY IN LONDON
CHESS 1495 (1965)

Chuck also had five tracks on the soundtrack album of the film 'Rock Rock Rock', released in 1958 on Chess 1425, almost concurrently with his own first solo album. 'Chuck Berry On Stage' was not an actual concert recording, but featured studio tracks with audience overdubbings.

ELVIS COSTELLO'S FIRST TEN SINGLES (UK RELEASES)

LESS THAN ZERO/Radio Sweetheart
Stiff BUY 11 (Mar. 1977)

ALISON/Welcome To The Working Week
Stiff BUY 14 (May 1977)

(THE ANGELS WANT TO WEAR MY RED SHOES/Mystery Dance
Stiff BUY 15 (Aug. 1977)

WATCHING THE DETECTIVES/ Blame It On Cain/Mystery Dance
Stiff BUY 20 (Oct. 1977)

(I DON'T WANT TO GO TO) CHELSEA/ You Belong To Me
Radar ADA 3 (Mar. 1978)

PUMP IT UP/Big Tears
Radar ADA 10 (Jun. 1978)

RADIO, RADIO/Tiny Steps
Radar ADA 24 (Oct. 1978)

OLIVER'S ARMY/My Funny Valentine
Radar ADA 31 (Jan. 1979)

ACCIDENTS WILL HAPPEN/ Talking In The Dark/Wednesday Week
Radar ADA 35 (Mar. 1979)

I CAN'T STAND UP FOR FALLING DOWN/Girls Talk
F-Beat XXI (Feb. 1980)

Costello's first chart entry, after much critical acclaim for his first three Stiff singles, was 'Watching The Detectives' at the end of 1977. After that, all the singles listed were big hits, and 'Oliver's Army' was a number one in the UK. 'I Can't Stand Up . . .', his first release on F-Beat, was originally scheduled to appear on the Specials' 2-Tone label and even allocated a catalogue number (CHS TT7), but it was never released in that form.

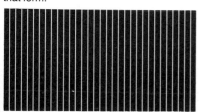

ELVIS COSTELLO'S FIRST TEN ALBUMS (UK RELEASES)

including compilation appearances

A BUNCH OF STIFFS
(various artists compilation)
SEEZ 2 (1977)

MY AIM IS TRUE
SEEZ 3 (1977)

LIVE STIFFS LIVE
(various artists compilation)
GET 1 (1977)

THIS YEAR'S MODEL
RAD 3 (1978)

HITS GREATEST STIFFS
(various artists compilation)
FIST 1 (1978)

ARMED FORCES
RAD 15 (1979)

AMERICATHON
(film soundtrack including
Costello tracks) CBS 70172 (1979)

MY VERY SPECIAL GUESTS
(George Jones album featuring a duet with Elvis on 'Stranger In The House'
EPC 83163 (1980)

GET HAPPY!
XXLP 1 (1980)

ALMOST BLUE
XXLP 13 (1981)

A further album which belongs in this sequence chronologically, but which was only released in the USA on the Columbia label, was 'Taking Liberties' (JC 36839), a collection of singles cuts and assorted rare tracks not to be found on other albums.

THE BEACH BOYS' FIRST TEN SINGLES (USA RELEASES)

SURFIN'/Luau
Candix 301 (Feb. 1962)
SURFIN' SAFARI/409
Capitol 4777 (May 1962)
TEN LITTLE INDIANS/County Fair
Capitol 4880 (Nov. 1962)
SURFIN' USA/Shut Down
Capitol 4932 (Mar. 1963)
SURFER GIRL/Little Deuce Coupe
Capitol 5009 (Jul. 1963)
**BE TRUE TO YOUR SCHOOL/
In My Room**
Capitol 5069 (Oct. 1963)
**LITTLE SAINT NICK/
The Lord's Prayer**
Capitol 5096 (Dec. 1963)
**FUN FUN FUN/
Why Do Fools Fall In Love?**
Capitol 5118 (Feb. 1964)
I GET AROUND/Don't Worry Baby
Capitol 5174 (May 1964)
**WHEN I GROW UP (TO BE A MAN)/
She Knows Me Too Well**
Capitol 5245 (Aug. 1964)

Candix was a California label, which nevertheless managed enough national distribution to lift the Beach Boys' 'Surfin' ' into the American top 100, where they were quickly noticed and signed up by Capitol. The subsequent nine releases included eight top 20 hits (including one B-side, 'Little Deuce Coupe'), and two million-sellers in 'Surfin' USA' and 'I Get Around'.

THE BEACH BOYS' FIRST TEN ALBUMS (USA RELEASES)

SURFIN' SAFARI
T 1808 (1962)
SURFIN' USA
T 1890 (1963)
SURFER GIRL
T 1981 (1963)
LITTLE DEUCE COUPE
SHUTDOWN, VOL. 2
T 2027 (1964)
T 1998 (1963)
ALL SUMMER LONG
T 2110 (1964)
THE BEACH BOYS' CHRISTMAS ALBUM
T 2164 (1964)
THE BEACH BOYS' CONCERT
T 2198 (1964)
THE BEACH BOYS TODAY
T 2269 (1965)
SUMMER DAYS (AND SUMMER NIGHTS!)
T 2354 (1965)

For their day, the Beach Boys had an incredibly prolific album output, quite unmatched by any other group of the era. However, some of these early albums were basically roundups of two or three succeeding singles plus 5 or 6 new tracks, while there were several track duplications across the second, third and fourth albums on the list.

THE FIRST TEN SINGLES ON THE SUN LABEL (USA RELEASES)

JOHNNY LONDON
DRIVIN' SLOW/Flat Tire
175

HANDY JACKSON
TROUBLE WILL GET YOU DOWN/
Got My Application
177

JOE HILL LOUIS
WE ALL GOTTA GO SOMETIME/
She May Be Yours
178

JIMMY AND WALTER
EASY/Before Long
179

WILLIE NIX
SEEMS LIKE A MILLION YEARS/
Baker Shop Boogie
180

RUFUS THOMAS
BEER CAT/Walking In the Rain
181

DUSTY BROOKS
HEAVEN OR FIRE/Tears And Wine
182

D.A. HUNT
LONESOME OLD JAIL/Greyhound
Blues
183

BIG MEMPHIS MARAINEY
CALL ME ANYTHING, BUT CALL ME/
Baby No No
184

JIMMY DeBERRY
TAKE A LITTLE CHANCE/
Time Has Made A Change
185

Sam Phillips' Sun label, based in
Memphis, Tennessee, was to discover
Elvis Presley, Jerry Lee Lewis, Johnny
Cash, Charlie Rich, Carl Perkins and Roy
Orbison. Its first releases, though, were
mostly straight blues or country records,
aimed at regional sales within those
particular markets. The ten singles listed
above were all released in the period
1953-54, though it is difficult to put
specific dates to them. Whilst most of the
names are unfamiliar except to blues
collectors, Rufus Thomas (who was a
Memphis DJ at the time) later became a
soul star of the sixties. 176 seems to
have not been issued, while the series as
a whole presumably started at 175
because Sun was a production company
before it became a label in its own right
(leasing out releases to other labels), and
the first 174 singles produced in the
studios were probably filed within the
company by those numbers.

THE FIRST TEN ALBUMS ON THE SUN LABEL (USA RELEASES)

Carl Perkins

Roy Orbison

Jerry Lee Lewis

JOHNNY CASH
WITH HIS HOT AND BLUE GUITAR
SLP 1220 (1957)

CARL PERKINS
TEEN BEAT
SLP 1225 (1957)

JERRY LEE LEWIS
JERRY LEE LEWIS
SLP 1230 (1958)

JOHNNY CASH
THE SONGS THAT MADE HIM FAMOUS
SLP 1235 (1959)

JOHNNY CASH
THE GREATEST
SLP 1240 (1959)

JOHNNY CASH
JOHNNY CASH SINGS HANK WILLIAMS
SLP 1245 (1960)

VARIOUS
SUN'S GOLDEN HITS
SLP 1250 (1960)

JOHNNY CASH
NOW HERE'S JOHNNY CASH!
SLP 1255 (1960)

ROY ORBISON
ROY AT THE ROCKHOUSE
SLP 1260 (1961)

JERRY LEE LEWIS
JERRY LEE'S GREATEST
SLP 1265 (1961)

Sun never did issue a vast quantity of albums (the number of subsequent reissue albums of Sun material must outnumber the originals by ten to one!), but those which did appear were hot compilations (mostly ex-singles cuts) by the label's biggest sellers. No Sun album was ever issued by Elvis Presley. The number sequence really did go up in fives!

THE FIRST TEN SINGLES ON THE PHILLES LABEL (USA RELEASES)

Ronnettes

CRYSTALS
THERE'S NO OTHER (LIKE MY BABY)/
Oh Yeah, Maybe Baby
100 (Nov. 1961)

JOEL SCOTT
HERE I STAND/You're My Only Love
101 (Dec. 1961)

CRYSTALS
UPTOWN/What A Nice Way
To Turn Seventeen
102 (Mar. 1962)

ALI HASSAN
CHOPSTICKS/Malaguena
103 (Apr. 1962)

STEVE DOUGLAS
LT. COLONEL BOGEY'S PARADE/
Yes Sir, That's My Baby
104 (Jun. 1962)

CRYSTALS
HE HIT ME (AND IT FELT LIKE
A KISS)/No One Ever Tells You
105 (Jul. 1962)

CRYSTALS
HE'S A REBEL/I Love You Eddie
106 (Aug. 1962)

BOB B SOXX
& THE BLUE JEANS
ZIP-A-DEE-DOO-DAH/Flip And Nitty
107 (Oct. 1962)

ALLEY CATS
PUDDIN' 'N' TAIN/Feel So Good
108 (Dec. 1962)

CRYSTALS
HE'S SURE THE BOY I LOVE/
Walkin' Along (La La La)
109 (Dec. 1962)

Phil Spector owned the Philles label and it was the home of most of his greatest productions like 'You've Lost That Lovin' Feelin' ' by the Righteous Brothers and 'Be My Baby' by the Ronettes. At the time of the first few releases he was still involved in freelance production work elsewhere (see listing of the first Spector-produced hit records), and 101, 103 and 104 on this list were produced by others – significantly, these records had no success at all, whereas almost every other item on the list stormed the US charts. The other exception was the Crystals' 'He Hit Me', withdrawn from the market after a few days because of radio objection to the lyrics; it was replaced by 'He's A Rebel', which gave Philles its first number one hit.

58

THE FIRST TEN ALBUMS ON THE PHILLES LABEL (USA RELEASES)

Bob B Soxx & The Blue Jeans

Crystals

CRYSTALS
TWIST UPTOWN
PHLP 4000 (1962)

CRYSTALS
HE'S A REBEL
PHLP 4001 (1963)

BOB B SOXX
& THE BLUE JEANS
ZIP-A-DEE-DOO-DAH
PHLP 4002 (1963)

CRYSTALS
THE CRYSTALS SING THE
GREATEST HITS
PHLP 4003 (1963)

VARIOUS
PHILLES RECORDS PRESENTS
TODAY'S HITS
PHLP 4004 (1963)

VARIOUS
A CHRISTMAS GIFT FOR YOU
PHLP 4005 (1963)

RONETTES
PRESENTING THE FABULOUS
RONETTES FEATURING VERONICA
PHLP 4006 (1964)

RIGHTEOUS BROTHERS
YOU'VE LOST THAT LOVIN' FEELIN'
PHLP 4007 (1965)

RIGHTEOUS BROTHERS
JUST ONCE IN MY LIFE
PHLP 4008 (1965)

RIGHTEOUS BROTHERS
BACK TO BACK
PHLP 4009 (1965)

The first two albums by the Crystals were almost identical in terms of song content. Presumably the first was pulled off the market to make way for the second, which replaced a couple of older tracks with newer hits. The most enduring Philles album release is 'A Christmas Gift For You', which has been reissued several times by different labels over the last eighteen years (usually under the title of 'Phil Spector's Christmas Album'), and still gets massive airplay each December.

THE FIRST TEN SINGLES ON THE ELEKTRA LABEL (USA)

Judy Collins

JUDY COLLINS
I'LL KEEP IT WITH MINE/
Thirsty Boots
45601

BAROQUE BEATLES BOOK
YOU'VE GOT TO HIDE YOUR
LOVE AWAY/Ticket To Ride
45602

LOVE
MY LITTLE RED BOOK/
A Message To Pretty
45603

TOM RUSH
ON THE ROAD AGAIN/
Why Do You Love?
45604

LOVE
7 AND 7 IS/Number Fourteen
45605

TIM BUCKLEY
WINGS/Grief In My Soul
45606

TOM RUSH
URGE FOR GOING/Sugar Babe
45607

LOVE
SHE COMES IN COLORS/
Orange Skies
45608

BUTTERFIELD BLUES BAND
COME ON IN/A Got A Mind To
Give Up Living
45609

JUDY COLLINS
HARD-LOVIN' LOSER/
I Think It's Going To Rain Today
45610

These were all released between November 1965 and January 1967, although precise dates of issue are difficult to pinpoint. Elektra's first American singles chart entry was Love's 'My Little Red Book' in May 1966, followed three months later by the same group's '7 and 7 Is'. A year after this, the Doors' 'Light My Fire' (45615) would give the label its first Number one hit.

THE FIRST TEN ALBUMS ON THE ELEKTRA LABEL (USA)

LOVE/
Love
74001

WHAT'S SHAKIN'
Lovin' Spoonful, Eric Clapton
and others
74002

DAVID BLUE
David Blue
74003

TIM BUCKLEY
Tim Buckley
74004

DA CAPO
Love
74005

BEATLE COUNTRY
Charles River Valley Boys
74006

THE DOORS
Doors
74007

THE ZODIAC COSMIC SOUNDS
Zodiac
74009

THE 5000 SPIRITS OR THE LAYERS OF THE ONION
Incredible String Band
74010

CLEAR LIGHT
Clear Light
74011

Album 74008 was apparently not released. Note Elektra's apparent obsession with eponymous album titles (see elsewhere in the book!) The Doors' debut album was the label's first really big seller, while the Incredible String Band represented the first release by a British act on the label.

THE FIRST TEN SINGLES ON THE DERAM LABEL (UK RELEASES)

Move

BEVERLEY
HAPPY NEW YEAR/Where the Good Times Are
DM 101 (Sept. 1966)

CAT STEVENS
I LOVE MY DOG/Portobello Road
DM 102 (Sept. 1966)

GIBSONS
TWO KINDS OF LOVERS/Hey Girl
DM 103 (Oct. 1966)

BARRY MASON
OVER THE HILLS AND FAR AWAY/Collections of Recollections
DM 104 (Oct. 66)

TRUTH
JINGLE-JANGLE/Hey Gyp
DM 105 (Nov. 1966)

EYES OF BLUE
UP AND DOWN/Heart Trouble
DM 106 (Nov. 1966)

DAVID BOWIE
RUBBER BAND/The London Boys
DM 107 (Dec. 1966)

CHIM KOTHARI
SITAR 'N' SPICE/Indian Bat
DM 108 (Dec. 1966)

MOVE
NIGHT OF FEAR/Disturbance
DM 109 (Dec. 1966)

CAT STEVENS
MATTHEW AND SON/Granny
DM 110 (Dec. 1966)

The Deram label was set up by the British giant Decca specifically to showcase new and young pop and rock talent. It struck immediate chart paydirt with Cat Stevens' 'I Love My Dog', failed to sell the David Bowie single, then had top ten hits with its ninth and tenth singles, becoming fully established. Big hits which followed soon after included follow-ups by the Move and Stevens, plus Procol Harum's 'A Whiter Shade of Pale', the Flowerpot Men's 'Let's Go To San Francisco', and 'I Was Kaiser Bill's Batman' by Whistling Jack Smith.

THE FIRST TEN ALBUMS ON THE DERAM LABEL (UK RELEASES)

Cat Stevens

vid Bowie

JOHNNY HOWARD
THE VELVET TOUCH OF
JOHNNY HOWARD
SML 1001 (1967)

CHIM KOTHARI
SOUND OF SITAR
SML 1002 (1967)

LOS ESCUDOS
NEW LOOK AT LATIN
SML 1003 (1967)

CAT STEVENS
MATTHEW AND SON
SML 1004 (1967)

GRAHAM COLLIER SEPTET
DEEP DARK BLUE CENTRE
SML 1005 (1967)

LEADING FIGURES
YESTERDAY'S SWINGERS FOR
TODAY
SML 1006 (1967)

DAVID BOWIE
DAVID BOWIE
SML 1007 (1967)

LES REED ORCHESTRA
FLY ME TO THE SUN
SML 1008 (1967)

WHISTLINIG JACK SMITH
AROUND THE WORLD
SML 1009 (1967)

ROBERTO MANN STRINGS & VOICES
THE GREAT WALTZES
SML 1010 (1967)

Considerably less interesting than the label's first set of singles, the albums veered towards stodgy MOR sets and odd esoteric items like 'Sound Of Sitar'. The first albums by Cat Stevens and David Bowie provide some interest, though: both releases are collectors' items today. The label also had some more interesting LPs on the way from the Moody Blues ('Days Of Future Passed'), Ten Years After and Amen Corner.

THE FIRST TEN SINGLES ON THE TAMLA MOTOWN LABEL (UK)

Stevie Wonder

The Supre

SUPREMES
STOP IN THE NAME OF LOVE/
I'm In Love Again
TMG 501 (Mar. 1965)

MARTHA & THE VANDELLAS
NOWHERE TO RUN/Motoring
TMG 502 (Mar. 1965)

MIRACLES
OOO BABY BABY/All That's Good
TMG 503 (Mar. 1965)

TEMPTATIONS
IT'S GROWING/
What Love Has Joined Together
TMG 504 (Mar. 1965)

STEVIE WONDER
KISS ME BABY/Tears In Vain
TMG 505 (Mar. 1965)

EARL VAN DYKE
ALL FOR YOU/
Too Many Fish In The Sea
TMG 506 (Mar. 1965)

FOUR TOPS
ASK THE LONELY/
Where Did You Go?
TMG 507 (Mar. 1965)

BRENDA HOLLOWAY
WHEN I'M GONE/
I've Been Good To You
TMG 508 (Apr. 1965)

JR. WALKER & THE ALL-STARS
SHOTGUN/Hot Cha
TMG 509 (Apr. 1965)

MARVIN GAYE
I'LL BE DOGGONE/
You've Been A Long Time Coming
TMG 510 (Apr. 1965)

Hardly can there have been a more
all-star line-up with which to start a label
– although surprisingly the singles by
Stevie Wonder, the Four Tops, the
Miracles, Marvin Gaye and Jr. Walker all
failed to chart in Britain, as all these
artists were still to establish their UK
credentials. Motown had previously been
licensed in Britain through a succession
of labels, including London-American,
Oriole, Fontana and Stateside, the last of
these deals bringing the first hit records,
including Mary Wells' 'My Guy' and 'Baby
Love' and 'Where Did Our Love Go' from
the Supremes.

THE FIRST TEN ALBUMS ON THE TAMLA MOTOWN LABEL (UK)

Four Tops

Marvin Gaye

VARIOUS – A COLLECTION OF 16 TAMLA MOTOWN HITS
TML 11001 (Apr. 1965)

SUPREMES
WITH LOVE (FROM US TO YOU)
TML 11002 (Apr. 1965)

MIRACLES
I LIKE IT LIKE THAT
TML 11003 (Apr. 1965)

MARVIN GAYE
HOW SWEET IT IS TO BE LOVED BY YOU
TML 11004 (Apr. 1965)

MARTHA & THE VANDELLAS
HEAT WAVE
TML 11005 (Apr. 1965)

MARY WELLS
MY BABY JUST CARES FOR ME
TML 11006 (Apr. 1965)

VARIOUS – THE MOTORTOWN REVUE
TML 11007 (May 1965)

MARVELETTES
THE MARVELLOUS MARVELETTES
TML 11008 (May 1965)

TEMPTATIONS
MEET THE TEMPTATIONS
TML 11009 (May 1965)

FOUR TOPS
THE FOUR TOPS
TML 11010 (Jun. 1965)

Note that 'Tamla Motown' kept that name in Britain until the late seventies, when it was abridged to Motown. The Motown Corporation in Detroit actually ran four major labels (Tamla, Motown, Gordy and Soul) plus a few smaller ones, which the British company collated under the one logo.

THE FIRST TEN SINGLES ON THE 2-TONE LABEL (UK RELEASES)

SPECIAL AKA/SELECTER
GANGSTERS/The Selecter
TT 1/2 (1979)

MADNESS
THE PRINCE/Madness
CHS TT 3 (1979)

SELECTER
ON MY RADIO/Too Much Pressure
CHS TT 4 (1979)

SPECIALS
A MESSAGE TO YOU RUDY/Nite Klub
CHS TT 5 (1979)

BEAT
THE TEARS OF A CLOWN/
Ranking Full Stop
CHS TT 6 (1979)

SPECIALS
THE SPECIALS AKA LIVE
(EP)/(Tracks): TOO MUCH TOO
YOUNG/Guns of Navarone/
Long Shot (Kick The Bucket)/The
Liquidator/Skinhead Moonstomp/
CHS TT 7 (1980)

SELECTER
THREE MINUTE HERO/James Bond
CHS TT 8 (1980)

BODY SNATCHERS
LET'S DO ROCK STEADY/
Ruder Than You
CHS TT 9 (1980)

SELECTER
MISSING WORDS/Carry Go Bring
Home
CHS TT 10 (1980)

SPECIALS
RAT RACE/Rude Boys Outa Jail
CHS TT 11 (1980)

The 2-Tone label, owned by the Specials and marketed by Chrysalis after the initial independent success of the first single (hence the addition of the CHS prefix), holds a record likely never to be beaten, in that it gained a high chart position in the UK with every one of its first ten singles. 'The Specials AKA Live' actually reached number one, one of the extremely select few extended play releases ever to do so.

THE FIRST ALBUMS ON THE 2-TONE LABEL (UK RELEASES)

SPECIALS/SPECIALS
CDL TT 5001 (1980)
SELECTER/THE SELECTER
CDL TT 5002 (1980)
SPECIALS/MORE SPECIALS
CDL TT 5003 (1981)
**VARIOUS – DANCE CRAZE/
(film soundtrack)**
CDL TT 5004 (1981)

Albums by other bands which were part
of the initial 2-Tone roster have since
been released by Stiff (Madness),
Go-Feet (The Beat) and Chrysalis (The
Selecter.)

THE FIRST TEN SINGLES ON THE STIFF LABEL (UK RELEASES)

Motorhead

NICK LOWE
SO IT GOES/Heart Of The City
BUY 1 (1976)

PINK FAIRIES
BETWEEN THE LINES/
Spoiling For A Fight
BUY 2 (1976)

ROOGALATOR
ALL ABROAD/Cincinnatti Fatback
BUY 3 (1976)

TYLA GANG
STYROFOAM/
Texas Chainsaw Massacre Boogie
BUY 4 (1976)

LEW LEWIS BAND
BOOGIE ON THE STREET/
Caravan Man
BUY 5 (1976)

DAMNED
NEW ROSE/Help
BUY 6 (1976)

RICHARD HELL & THE VOIDOIDS
ANOTHER WORLD/Blank
Generation/You Gotta Lose
BUY 7 (1976)

PLUMMET AIRLINES
SILVER SHIRT/This Is The World
BUY 8 (1976)

MOTORHEAD
LEAVIN' HERE/White Line Fever
BUY 9 (1977)

DAMNED
NEAT NEAT NEAT/Stab Your
Back/Singalonga Scabies
BUY 10 (1977)

The Motorhead single, although
scheduled with the above catalogue
number, failed to appear in the
chronological sequence. Only a couple of
years later, when all ten of these singles
were reissued as a limited edition boxed
set, did it turn up with the others. The
Roogalator single (BUY 3) played at
33⅓rpm (normally album speed) rather
than 45. Although none of the above
singles made the charts, Stiff was
undoubtedly the most successful of the
early breed of new independent labels
which sprang up in Britain during the late
1970s. Its charisma and quality of
material brought it critical acclaim and
regular publicity long before big sales,
but with the advent of Elvis Costello and
Ian Dury just a few releases after those
above, there was no looking back.

THE FIRST TEN ALBUMS ON THE STIFF LABEL

Nick Lowe

DAMNED
DAMNED, DAMNED, DAMNED
SEEZ 1 (1977)

VARIOUS – A BUNCH OF STIFFS
SEEZ 2 (1977)

ELVIS COSTELLO
MY AIM IS TRUE
SEEZ 3 (1977)

IAN DURY & THE BLOCKHEADS
NEW BOOTS AND PANTIES!
SEEZ 4 (1977)

DAMNED
MUSIC FOR PLEASURE
SEEZ 5 (1977)

WRECKLESS ERIC
WRECKLESS ERIC
SEEZ 6 (1978)

VARIOUS – HITS GREATEST STIFFS
FIST 1 (1978)

VARIOUS – LIVE STIFFS LIVE
GET 1 (1978)

LENE LOVICH
STATELESS
SEEZ 7 (1978)

JONA LEWIE
ON THE OTHER HAND
THERE'S A FIST
SEEZ 8 (1978)

The Costello and Dury albums sold in vast quantities, effectively subsidising the rest of the releases. The former was partially remixed and had a track ('Watching The Detectives') added for its American release, while the latter was also pressed in a special limited edition gold vinyl form with 'Sex And Drugs And Rock & Roll' added as a bonus track. Catalogue number was SEEZ G4. Wreckless Eric's album also appeared in a 10-inch brown vinyl edition, numbered SEEZ B6.

THE FIRST TEN SINGLES ON THE VIRGIN LABEL (UK RELEASES)

Link Wray

TUBULAR BELLS
Mike Oldfield
VS 101

MARLENE
Kevin Coyne
VS 102

I'M SO GLAD, I'M SO PROUD/Shawnee Tribe
Link Wray
VS 103

LOVESICK FOOL/Sea Of Love
Kevin Coyne
VS 104

CASA BLANCA MOON/Slow Moons Rose
Slap Happy
VS 105

VS 106

I BELIEVE IN LOVE
Kevin Coyne

VS 107

HIGH SCHOOL/Sunrise
Chili Charles
VS 108

YOU'RE THE ONLY ONE
Carol Grimes
VS 109

VS 110

VS 111

VS 112

Virgin, though now an energetic but familiar part of the British rock mainstream, was quite an esoteric label in its earliest years. Singles came about as something of an afterthought once the LP series had been firmly established with Mike Oldfield's 'Tubular Bells', but it was appropriate that Oldfield should start off the singles list too. The 'Tubular Bells' excerpt on single was used in the USA as theme for the film 'The Exorcist'.

THE FIRST TEN ALBUMS ON THE VIRGIN LABEL

Tangerine Dream

Kevin Coyne

TUBULAR BELLS
Mike Oldfield
(1973)
V 2001

**RADIO GNOME INVISIBLE, PART 1:
THE FLYING TEAPOT**
Gong
(1973)
V 2002

MANOR LIVE
Various
(1973)
V 2003

FAUST 4
Faust
V 2004

THE HENRY COW LEGEND
Henry Cow
(1973)
V 2005

BEANS AND FATBACK
Link Wray
(1973)
V 2006

**RADIO GNOME INVISIBLE, PART 2:
ANGEL'S EGG**
Gong
(1973)
V 2007

**THE HATFIELD AND THE NORTH
ALBUM**
Hatfield And The North
(1974)
V 2008

BUSY CORNER
Chili Charles
(1974)
V 2009

PHAEDRA
Tangerine Dream
(1974)
V 2010

Apart from the all-conquering 'Tubular Bells' the albums offered further musical esoterica, of the kind associated more with independent labels of the Rough Trade variety a few years later. Other artists soon to turn up on Virgin included Captain Beefheart, David Bedford, Kevin Coyne and Robert Wyatt while Mike Oldfield had two more huge sellers in 'Hergest Ridge' and 'Ommadawn'.

THE FIRST TEN SINGLES ON THE APPLE LABEL (UK RELEASES)

Mary Hopkin

BEATLES
HEY JUDE/Revolution
R 5722 (Aug. 1968)

MARY HOPKIN
THOSE WERE THE DAYS/
Turn Turn Turn
2 (Aug. 1968)

JACKIE LOMAX
SOUR MILK SEA/The Eagle Laughs At You
3 (Aug. 1968)

BLACK DYKE MILLS BAND
THINGUMYBOB/Yellow Submarine
4 (Aug. 1968)

IVEYS
MAYBE TOMORROW/And Her Daddy's A Millionaire
5 (Jan. 1969)

TRASH
ROAD TO NOWHERE/Illusions
6 (Mar. 1969)

MARY HOPKIN
GOODBYE/Sparrow
10 (Apr. 1969)

BEATLES
GET BACK/Don't Let Me Down
R 5777 (Apr. 1969)

JACKIE LOMAX
NEW DAY/(I) Fall Inside Your Eyes
11 (May 1969)

BEATLES
THE BALLAD OF JOHN AND YOKO/
Old Brown Shoe
R 5786 (May 1969)

This very odd number sequence needs some clarification. Although the Beatles owned the Apple label, they were themselves contracted to EMI. This led to their releases appearing with Apple labels, but bearing EMI Parlophone catalogue numbers. Therefore, although 'Hey Jude' was indeed the first Apple single, there never actually was an Apple 1. The missing numbers 7, 8 and 9 do exist, but they were pressed for export markets only and not released in the UK. 7 and 9 were Italian and French-language singles by Mary Hopkin, while 8 was the banned 'King of Fuh' by Brute Force (banned because the lyrics mentioned the Fuh King, and it sounded like something different.)

THE FIRST TEN
ALBUMS ON
THE APPLE LABEL
(UK RELEASES)

Billy Preston

George Harrison

BEATLES
THE BEATLES (THE WHITE ALBUM)
PCS 7067/8 (Nov. 1968)

GEORGE HARRISON
WONDERWALL MUSIC
SAPCOR 1 (Nov. 1968)

JOHN LENNON & YOKO ONO
TWO VIRGINS
SAPCOR 2 (Nov. 1968)

BEATLES/FILM SOUNDTRACK
YELLOW SUBMARINE
PCS 7070 (Dec. 1968)

JAMES TAYLOR
JAMES TAYLOR
SAPCOR 3 (Feb. 1969)

MODERN JAZZ QUARTET
UNDER THE JASMIN TREE
SAPCOR 4 (Feb. 1969)

MARY HOPKIN
POSTCARD
SAPCOR 5 (Mar. 1969)

JACKIE LOMAX
IS THIS WHAT YOU WANT?
SAPCOR 6 (May 1969)

IVEYS
MAYBE TOMORROW
SAPCOR 8 (Jun. 1969)

BILLY PRESTON
THAT'S THE WAY GOD PLANNED IT
SAPCOR 9 (Sept. 1969)

See notes on the singles to explain the
odd number sequence. SAPCOR 7 was
not released, but was originally
scheduled to be either 'White Trash' by
Trash, or 'Accept No Substitute' by
Delaney & Bonnie, depending upon
whose story you believe. The Delaney &
Bonnie album eventually turned up on the
Elektra label.

THE ARTISTS IN THE FIRST-EVER BRITISH TOP TEN

Doris Day

1 **ROSEMARY CLOONEY**
(with **Half As Much**)

2 **NAT 'KING' COLE**
(with **Somewhere Along The Way**)

3 **BING CROSBY**
(with **Isle of Innisfree**)

4 **DORIS DAY & FRANKIE LAINE**
(with **Sugarbush**)

5 **FRANKIE LAINE**
(with **High Noon**)

6 **VERA LYNN**
(with **Auf Weidersehen Sweetheart**)

7 **RAY MARTIN**
(with **Blue Tango**)

8 **AL MARTINO**
(with **Here In My Heart**)

9 **GUY MITCHELL**
(with **Feet Up (Pat Him On The Po-Po)**)

10 **JO STAFFORD**
(with **You Belong To Me**)

Al Martino had the first UK number one hit with 'Here In My Heart'; it was eventually displaced by Jo Stafford's 'You Belong To Me', which stood at 2 first week out. Vera Lynn's 'Auf Weidersehen' had been an American chart-topper earlier in the year, and obviously would have performed likewise in Britain, had the chart been in existence a couple of months earlier. Apart perhaps from orchestra leader Ray Martin (who nonetheless had a couple more British hits), all the names here continued to be familiar record sellers for many years. Nat Cole and Bing Crosby are now deceased, of course, while only Martino, Lynn and Laine seem to have actively recorded into the 1980s.

The songs in that first chart generally wore less well than their performers. 'You Belong To Me' has had a couple of hit revivals through the years, but probably the best-remembered number nowadays is 'High Noon' ('Do Not Forsake Me, Oh My Darling. . .'), because of occasional TV revivals of the famous film of which it is the title song.

74

THE ACTS IN THE FIRST-EVER AMERICAN TOP TEN

(20th July, 1940 – from Billboard)

TOMMY DORSEY (twice)
GLENN MILLER (four times)
JIMMY DORSEY
BING CROSBY
KAY KYSER
MITCHELL AYRES

One of Tommy Dorsey's two entries was the number one song, 'I'll Never Smile Again' – the first-ever chart-topping single. Note the total big-band domination; Glenn Miller actually had eleven top ten hits during that second six months of 1940, while Tommy Dorsey had seven and brother Jimmy just two. Of the two unfamiliar names in the list, Kay Kyser (who stood at No. 4 with 'Playmates') actually had about 20 more hits through the next eight years – but spare a thought for Mitchell Ayres. From holding the No. 10 slot in that first-ever chart with 'Make-Believe Island', he vanished the following week and has never appeared in any chart since during the last 41 years!

THE ACTS IN THE FIRST-EVER BBC-TV TOP OF THE POPS' SHOW

Jimi Hendrix

1 TOM PAXTON
2 AMERICA
3 LESLEY DUNCAN
4 ALICE COOPER
5 ALICE STUART
6 BILL HALEY & THE COMETS
7 CLYDE McPHATTER
8 JIMI HENDRIX
9 BOB DYLAN
10 IAN WHITCOMB (the host)

THE ACTS ON THE FIRST-EVER BBC-TV 'OLD GREY WHISTLE TEST' SHOW

Holli

The BBC's two most enduring popular music shows, both catering for distinctly different parts of the audience, and both looking like running forever in basically the same formats. 'TOTP' revolves closely the acts in the upper reaches of the current week's singles chart, while 'OGWT' features more serious rock acts playing live (though without an audience) in the studio, plus film and archive items. 'Old Grey Whistle Test', incidentally, is a piece of music publishing jargon from way back – when elderly or greying men could be heard whistling a new tune in the street, the publisher knew he had a hit!

1 DUSTY SPRINGFIELD
2 ROLLING STONES
3 DAVE CLARK FIVE
4 HOLLIES
5 SWINGING BLUE JEANS
6 DENISE SAMPEY (the girl who spun the records for Jimmy Savile)
7 CLIFF RICHARD and the SHADOWS
8 FREDDIE & THE DREAMERS
9 BEATLES
10 JIMMY SAVILE (the DJ)

HISTORIC 'FIRSTS' IN THE RECORD INDUSTRY

1 1877 – Thomas Edison's cylinder 'Phonograph'.

2 1886 – Alexander Graham Bell's 'Graphophone', using wax cylinders.

3 1887 – The first record company – the American Graphophone Co. of Bridgeport, Connecticut.

4 1888 – The flat recording disc make of zinc, invented by Emile Berliner.

5 1896 – The first clockwork-driven wind-up gramophones.

6 1903 – The first million-selling record, 'Vesti La Giubba' by Enrico Caruso, recorded

7 1917 – The first jazz band recordings.

8 1923 – The first field recordings of American Hillbilly music, which would one day become Country & Western.

9 1925 – The first electrical recordings using a microphone.

10 1940 – The first record charts in the USA.

11 1948 – The first LP records on microgroove vinyl.

12 1952 – The first record charts in the UK.

13 1954 – Elvis Presley starts recording for Sun Records, Memphis.

14 1955 – The fully-fledged arrival of rock'n'roll music.

15 1958 – The first stereo albums.

16 1961 – The Beatles start recording for Polydor Records, Hamburg.

17 1964 – Conquest of the musical world by the Beatles and British rock.

18 1965 – The first musicassettes, developed in Europe.

19 1970 – The first equipment and recordings for quadrophonic sound, which proves to be an expensive white elephant within a decade.

20 1980 – The first domestic video discs introduced in the USA.

The first recording ever made, by Thomas Alva Edison on his Phonograph with its tinfoil-wrapped cylinder, was of 'Mary Had A Little Lamb', spoken in the inventors' own voice. This occurred on the 15th August 1877, a date notable for its NON-celebration by the recording industry in 1977, a hundred years later. The first instrumental performance on the Edison cylinder was by a boy pianist named Josef Hoffman in 1888.

THE FIRST TEN AMERICAN HIT RECORDS PRODUCED BY PHIL SPECTOR

Phil Spector

The Teddy Bears with Phil Spector

1 **TO KNOW HIM IS TO LOVE HIM**
Teddy Bears
(charted Sept. 1958 – reached 1)

2 **CORRINA, CORRINA**
Ray Peterson
(charted Nov. 1960 – reached 9)

3 **PRETTY LITTLE ANGEL EYES**
Curtis Lee
(charted Jul. 1961 – reached 7)

4 **EVERY BREATH I TAKE**
Gene Pitney
(charted Aug. 1961 – reached 42)

5 **I LOVE HOW YOU LOVE ME**
Paris Sisters
(charted Sept. 1961 – reached 5)

6 **UNDER THE MOON OF LOVE**
Curtis Lee
(charted Oct. 1961 – reached 46)

7 **THERE'S NO OTHER (LIKE MY BABY)**
Crystals
(charted Nov. 1961 – reached 20)

8 **HE KNOWS I LOVE HIM TOO MUCH**
Paris Sisters
(charted Jan. 1962 – reached 34)

9 **UPTOWN**
Crystals
(charted Mar. 1962 – reached 13)

10 **SECOND HAND LOVE**
Connie Francis
(charted May 1962 – reached 7)

Spector was a member of the one-girl, two-boy trio known as the Teddy Bears when he was only 17 years old. After that first massive success he turned to songwriting and production, and upon completing some two years of 'learning the ropes', entered the period of freelance production assignments which gave him most of the string of hits listed above. By the end of 1961, he had established the credentials he needed to start his own label, Philles Records (named for Phil and his partner *Les*ter Sill), and the two Crystals records shown above were his first two productions for it. Subsequent successes came from the Ronettes, Bob B Soxx & The Blue Jeans, the Righteous Brothers and Ike & Tina Turner, and the Spector production 'sound' became a legend.

THE FIRST TEN BRITISH HIT RECORDS PRODUCED BY JOE MEEK

Mike Berry & The Original Outlaws

1 **GREEN JEANS**
Flee-Rekkers
(charted May 7th 1960 – reached 26)

2 **ANGELA JONES**
Michael Cox
(charted Jun. 11th 1960 – reached 8)

3 **ALONG CAME CAROLINE**
Michael Cox
(charted Oct. 1st 1960 – reached 30)

4 **SWINGIN' LOW**
Outlaws
(charted Apr. 15th 1961 – reached 46)

5 **AMBUSH**
Outlaws
(charted Jun. 10th 1961 – reached 43)

6 **JOHNNY REMEMBER ME**
John Leyton
(charted Aug. 5th 1961 – reached 1)

7 **WILD WIND**
John Leyton
(charted Oct. 7th 1961 – reached 2)

8 **TRIBUTE TO BUDDY HOLLY**
Mike Berry
(charted Oct. 14th 1961 – reached 23)

9 **NIGHT OF THE VAMPIRE**
Moontrekkers
(charted Nov. 4th 1961 – reached 50)

10 **SON, THIS IS SHE**
John Leyton
(charted Dec. 30th 1961 – reached 12)

Joe Meek was the original charismatic British independent record producer, placing his distinctive 'stamp' – heavy use of overdub, echo, compression, and unusual sounds – upon every record. He created all his hits in a tiny studio/flat in Holloway Road, with the echo chamber in the bathroom, etc.

The first two hits on this list were on Meek's own Triumph label, but during 1960 he adopted a policy of leasing his RGM Sound Productions to major UK labels, which was how the remainder of the titles on this list appeared. His greatest achievements came in 1962 with the Tornados' world-wide chart topper 'Telstar', and two years later with The Honeycombs' transatlantic smash 'Have I The Right'. Meek became a disillusioned man, out of tune with the sound of the times, during the mid-sixties, and finally committed suicide in mysterious circumstances, early in 1967.

Gerry and the Pacemakers

GERRY PACEMAKERS 3

Don't
Let
The
Sun
Catch
You
Crying

S · GERRY'S HITS · G

I LIKE IT
Words and music by
MITCH MURRAY

I like it, I like it
I like the way you run your fingers thro' my
hair
And I like the way you tickle my chin
And I like the way you let me come in
When your mother ain't there.

I like it, I like it
I like the words you say and all the things you do
And I like the way you straighten my tie
And I like the way you're winkin' your eye
And I know I like you—you know I like you.

Do that again
You're driving me insane
Kiss me once more
That's another thing I like you for.

I like it, I like it
I like the funny feeling being here with you
And I like it more with every day
And I like it always hearing you say
You're liking it too—you're liking it too.

I'm asking you
What do you wanna do
Do you agree
That the world was made for you and me.

I like it, I like it,
I like the funny feeling being here with you
And I like it more with every day
And I like it always hearing you say
You're liking it too—you're liking it too.
Whoa, I like it. Are you liking it too?

Released on 4th May, 1963. Words
reproduced by permission of Jaep
Music, Ltd.

11

THE FIRST TWENTY MERSEYBEAT CHART HITS IN THE UK

1 **LOVE ME DO**
Beatles
(charted Oct. 13th 1962 – reached 21)

2 **PLEASE PLEASE ME**
Beatles
(charted Jan. 19th 1963 – reached 1)

3 **HOW DO YOU DO IT?**
Gerry & The Pacemakers
(charted Mar. 16th 1963 – reached 1)

4 **SOME OTHER GUY**
Big Three
(charted Apr. 13th 1963 – reached 29)

5 **FROM ME TO YOU**
Beatles
(charted Apr. 20th 1963 – reached 1)

6 **DO YOU WANT TO KNOW A SECRET?**
Billy J Kramer & The Dakotas
(charted May 4th 1963 – reached 1)

7 **IF YOU GOTTA MAKE A FOOL OF SOMEBODY**
Freddie & The Dreamers
(charted May 11th 1963 – reached 2)

8 **I LIKE IT**
Gerry & The Pacemakers
(charted Jun. 1st 1963 – reached 1)

9 **(AIN'T THAT) JUST LIKE ME**
Hollies
(charted Jun. 1st 1963 – reached 30)

10 **IT'S TOO LATE NOW**
Swinging Blue Jeans
(charted Jun. 22nd 1963 – reached 30)

11 **SWEETS FOR MY SWEET**
Searchers
(charted Jun. 29th 1963 – reached 1)

12 **BY THE WAY**
Big Three
(charted Jul. 6th 1963 – reached 23)

13 **THE CRUEL SEA**
Dakotas
(charted Jul. 13th 1963 – reached 16)

14 **TWIST AND SHOUT (EP)**
Beatles
(charted Jul. 20th 1963 – reached 3)

15 **BAD TO ME**
Billy J Kramer & The Dakotas
(charted Aug. 3rd – reached 1)

16 **HOW DO YOU DO IT? (EP)**
Gerry & The Pacemakers
(charted Aug. 3rd 1963 – reached 36)

17 **I'M TELLING YOU NOW**
Freddie & The Dreamers
(charted Aug. 10th 1963 – reached 2)

18 **SEARCHIN'**
Hollies
(charted Aug. 31st 1963 – reached 16)

19 **BE MY GIRL**
Dennisons
(charted Aug. 31st 1963 – reached 46)

20 **SHE LOVES YOU**
Beatles
(charted Aug. 31st 1963 – reached 1)

A measure of the thoroughness with which the groups from the North-West corner of Britain took over the UK singles charts during 1963, is that once 'Please Please Me' had taken the Beatles to the top, a remarkable percentage of the singers listed here went all the way to the number one or two slot. Gerry & The Pacemakers and Billy J Kramer & The Dakotas each reached the top with their first two singles, while Freddie & The Dreamers took their first two to the runner-up slot. Oddly, the Big Three, the third Liverpool group to make the charts, were never to reap the same sort of benefits as most of the others; 'By The Way' at a fairly lowly position 23 was the biggest hit they had.

Interesting to see that Gerry & The Pacemakers were so hot by August that an EP containing both sides of their first two singles managed to climb to 36 in its own right – despite the fact that the second of these singles ('I Like It') was still in the top 20 at the time!

SECTION 2

BEST SELLERS

THE TWENTY WORLDWIDE ALL-TIME BEST-SELLING SINGLES

Bing Crosby

Wings

1 **WHITE CHRISTMAS**
Bing Crosby
(over 30 million)

2 **ROCK AROUND THE CLOCK**
Bill Haley & The Comets
(over 17 million)

3 **I WANT TO HOLD YOUR HAND**
Beatles
(over 12 million)

4 **IT'S NOW OR NEVER**
Elvis Presley
(over 10 million)

5 **HOUND DOG/DON'T BE CRUEL**
Elvis Presley
(over 9 million)

6 **I'M A BELIEVER**
Monkees
(over 8 million)

7 **DIANA**
Paul Anka
(over 9 million)

8 **HEY JUDE**
Beatles
(over 8 million)

9 **THOSE WERE THE DAYS**
Mary Hopkin
(over 8 million)

10 **RUDOLPH THE RED-NOSED REINDEER**
Gene Autry
(over 7 million)

11 **SILENT NIGHT/ADESTE FIDELES**
Bing Crosby
(over 7 million)

12 **CAN'T BUY ME LOVE**
Beatles
(over 6 million)

13 **SUGAR SUGAR**
Archies
(over 6 million)

14 **MULL OF KINTYRE**
Wings
(over 6 million)

Village People

15 **YOU'RE THE ONE THAT I WANT**
   John Travolta & Olivia
   Newton-John
   (over 6 million)

16 **YOU LIGHT UP MY LIFE**
   Debby Boone
   (over 6 million)

17 **SHE LOVES YOU**
   Beatles
   (over 6 million)

18 **I'LL BE THERE**
   Jackson 5
   (over 6 million)

19 **PAPER DOLL**
   Mills Brothers
   (over 6 million)

20 **YMCA**
   Village People
   (over 6 million)

'White Christmas' has been going strong for 40-odd years now, and is so far ahead of every other single ever released in terms of worldwide sales, that it seems inconceivable that it could be caught up by anything else. Because it is the classic secular Christmas song, it is an automatic seller every Christmas and looks likely to continue that way for the foreseeable future. Likewise, 'Rock Around The Clock', as the archetypal rock'n'roll hit, has always been in steady demand; likewise the Presley and Beatles titles, which constantly benefit from new generations of fans coming late to these two major shapers of rock music.

THE THIRTY BIGGEST-SELLING SINGLES OF THE 1950s IN THE USA

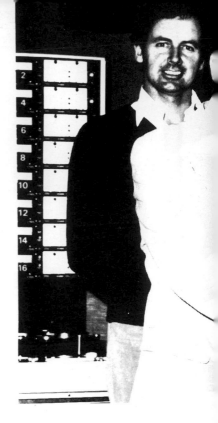

1 **DON'T BE CRUEL/HOUND DOG**
   Elvis Presley
   (1956)

2 **LOVE LETTERS IN THE SAND**
   Pat Boone
   (1957)

3 **ROCK AROUND THE CLOCK**
   Bill Haley & The Comets
   (1954)

4 **THE CHIPMUNK SONG (CHRISTMAS DON'T BE LATE)**
   Chipmunks
   (1958)

5 **TOM DOOLEY**
   Kingston Trio
   (1958)

6 **LOVE ME TENDER**
   Elvis Presley
   (1956)

7 **DIANA**
   Paul Anka
   (1957)

8 **TENNESSEE WALTZ**
   Patti Page
   (1950)

9 **JAILHOUSE ROCK**
   Elvis Presley
   (1957)

10 **VOLARE (NEL BLU DIPINTU DI BLU)**
   Domenico Modugno
   (1958)

11 **ALL SHOOK UP**
   Elvis Presley
   (1957)

12 **TEDDY BEAR**
   Elvis Presley
   (1957)

13 **(HOW MUCH IS THAT) DOGGIE IN THE WINDOW?**
   Patti Page
   (1953)

14 **HEARTBREAK HOTEL**
   Elvis Presley
   (1956)

15 **SINGING THE BLUES**
   Guy Mitchell
   (1956)

16 **CATCH A FALLING STAR/ MAGIC MOMENTS**
   Perry Como
   (1958)

17 **MACK THE KNIFE**
   Bobby Darin
   (1959)

18 **CRY/THE LITTLE WHITE CLOUD THAT CRIED**
   Johnnie Ray
   (1951)

19 **A FOOL SUCH AS I**
   Elvis Presley
   (1959)

20 **THIS OLE HOUSE**
   Rosemary Clooney
   (1954)

21 **IT'S ALL IN THE GAME**
   Tommy Edwards
   (1958)

Bill Haley

22 TOO MUCH
   Elvis Presley
   (1957)

23 THE HARRY LIME THEME
   (THE THIRD MAN)
   Anton Karas
   (1950)

24 I SAW MOMMY KISSING
   SANTA CLAUS
   Jimmy Boyd
   (1952)

25 SIXTEEN TONS
   Tennessee Ernie Ford
   (1955)

26 A BIG HUNK O' LOVE
   Elvis Presley
   (1959)

27 MONA LISA
   Nat 'King' Cole
   (1950)

28 DON'T
   Elvis Presley
   (1958)

29 I BELIEVE
   Frankie Laine
   (1953)

30 GOODNIGHT IRENE
   Weavers
   (1950)

It is probably superfluous to say that record sales in the 1950s were dominated by the success of Elvis Presley; the evidence is that he holds 10 of the 30 places on this listing, including the top slot. 'Don't Be Cruel'/'Hound Dog' sold over five million copies, making it far and away the biggest disc of the decade; the two sides lined up at numbers 1 and 2 on the American singles chart for more than two months, outselling individually (never mind collectively) everything else the industry could bring to bear. Johnnie Ray's huge double-sider at number 18 in the list had achieved the same trick in 1951, although not with sales of the same magnitude.

THE THIRTY BIGGEST-SELLING SINGLES OF THE 1960s IN THE UK

Tom Jones

1 SHE LOVES YOU
   Beatles
   (1963)

2 I WANT TO HOLD YOUR HAND
   Beatles
   (1963)

3 TEARS
   Ken Dodd
   (1965)

4 CAN'T BUY ME LOVE
   Beatles
   (1964)

5 I FEEL FINE
   Beatles
   (1964)

6 THE CARNIVAL IS OVER
   Seekers
   (1965)

7 WE CAN WORK IT OUT/
   DAY TRIPPER
   Beatles
   (1965)

8 RELEASE ME
   Engelbert Humperdinck
   (1967)

9 IT'S NOW OR NEVER
   Elvis Presley
   (1960)

10 GREEN GREEN GRASS OF HOME
   Tom Jones
   (1966)

11 THE LAST WALTZ
   Engelbert Humperdinck
   (1967)

12 I REMEMBER YOU
   Frank Ifield
   (1962)

13 STRANGER ON THE SHORE
   Mr Acker Bilk
   (1961)

14 THE YOUNG ONES
   Cliff Richard
   (1962)

15 SUGAR SUGAR
   Archies
   (1969)

16 THE NEXT TIME/BACHELOR BOY
   Cliff Richard
   (1962)

17 TELSTAR
   Tornados
   (1962)

18 HELP
   Beatles
   (1965)

19 TWO LITTLE BOYS
   Rolf Harris
   (1969)

20 GLAD ALL OVER
   Dave Clark Five
   (1963)

21 NEEDLES AND PINS
   Searchers
   (1964)

The Rolling Stones

The Searchers

Rolf Harris

22 ANYONE WHO HAD A HEART
Cilla Black
(1964)

23 LOVESICK BLUES
Frank Ifield
(1962)

24 HEY JUDE
Beatles
(1968)

25 I LOVE YOU BECAUSE
Jim Reeves
(1964)

26 YOU'LL NEVER WALK ALONE
Gerry & The Pacemakers
(1963)

27 THERE GOES MY EVERYTHING
Engelbert Humperdinck
(1967)

28 I WON'T FORGET YOU
Jim Reeves
(1964)

29 A HARD DAY'S NIGHT
Beatles
(1964)

30 THE LAST TIME
Rolling Stones
(1965)

The Beatles conquered British pop music in the sixties, and have appropriately had more million-selling singles in the UK (five) than any other act. All the top fourteen titles on this list reached seven-figures on UK sales alone, and until Wings' 'Mull of Kintyre' came along, 'She Loves You' remained as Britain's all-time best-selling single for fourteen years. It continues to sell today, along with a significant number of other titles from this list which remain in catalogue.

THE THIRTY BIGGEST-SELLING SINGLES OF THE 1960s IN THE USA

Louis Armstrong

1 I WANT TO HOLD YOUR HAND
Beatles
(1964)

2 THE BALLAD OF THE GREEN BERETS
S. Sgt. Barry Sadler
(1966)

3 IT'S NOW OR NEVER
Elvis Presley
(1960)

4 HEY JUDE
Beatles
(1968)

5 LOVE IS BLUE
Paul Mauriat
(1967)

6 HARPER VALLEY P.T.A.
Jeannie C Riley
(1968)

7 I'M A BELIEVER
Monkees
(1966)

8 I HEARD IT THROUGH THE GRAPEVINE
Marvin Gaye
(1968)

9 SUGAR SUGAR
Archies
(1969)

10 HONEY
Bobby Goldsboro
(1968)

11 CAN'T BUY ME LOVE
Beatles
(1964)

12 SHE LOVES YOU
Beatles
(1964)

13 THE TWIST
Chubby Checker
(1960)

14 CRIMSON AND CLOVER
Tommy James & The Shondells
(1968)

15 THE LETTER
Box Tops
(1967)

16 AQUARIUS/LET THE SUNSHINE IN
5th Dimension
(1969)

17 I CAN'T STOP LOVING YOU
Ray Charles
(1962)

18 I WANT YOU BACK
Jackson 5
(1969)

19 RAINDROPS KEEP FALLIN' ON MY HEAD
B.J. Thomas
(1969)

20 GET BACK
Beatles
(1969)

The 5th Dimension

21 IN THE YEAR 2525
(EXORDIUM AND TERMINUS)
Zager And Evans
(1969)

22 ODE TO BILLIE JOE
Bobbie Gentry
(1967)

23 ARE YOU LONESOME TONIGHT?
Elvis Presley
(1960)

24 TO SIR WITH LOVE
Lulu
(1967)

25 DAYDREAM BELIEVER
Monkees
(1967)

26 THEME FROM 'A SUMMER
PLACE'
Percy Faith
(1960)

27 LOVE CHILD
Diana Ross & The Supremes
(1968)

28 HELLO DOLLY
Louis Armstrong
(1964)

29 GREEN TAMBOURINE
Lemon Pipers
(1967)

30 I FEEL FINE
Beatles
(1964)

While the 1950s belonged to Elvis, the 60s just as surely danced to the Beatles' tune. The Fab Four have six of these 30 top sellers, including the number one 'I Want To Hold Your Hand', which sold five million copies in the USA alone. Considering that the 60s are remembered as the decade in which British artists conquered America, it's perhaps a little surprising that apart from the Beatles' discs, the only British record showing here is Lulu's 'To Sir With Love'.

THE THIRTY BIGGEST-SELLING SINGLES OF THE 1970s IN THE UK

1 MULL OF KINTYRE
  Wings
  (1977)

2 RIVERS OF BABYLON/
  BROWN GIRL IN THE RING
  Boney M
  (1978)

3 YOU'RE THE ONE THAT I WANT
  John Travolta & Olivia
  Newton-John
  (1978)

4 MARY'S BOY CHILD/OH MY LORD
  Boney M
  (1978)

5 SUMMER NIGHTS
  John Travolta & Olivia
  Newton-John
  (1978)

6 BRIGHT EYES
  Art Garfunkel
  (1979)

7 YMCA
  Village People
  (1978)

8 BOHEMIAN RHAPSODY
  Queen
  (1975)

9 ANOTHER BRICK IN THE WALL
  Pink Floyd
  (1979)

10 HEART OF GLASS
  Blondie
  (1979)

11 I LOVE YOU LOVE ME LOVE
  Gary Glitter
  (1973)

12 DON'T GIVE UP ON US
  David Soul
  (1976)

13 SAVE YOUR KISSES FOR ME
  Brotherhood Of Man
  (1976)

14 IMAGINE
  John Lennon
  (1975)

Wi...

15 MERRY XMAS EVERYBODY
  Slade
  (1973)

16 EYE LEVEL
  Simon Park Orchestra
  (1972)

17 LONG-HAIRED LOVER
  FROM LIVERPOOL
  Little Jimmy Osmond
  (1972)

18 I'D LIKE TO TEACH THE
  WORLD TO SING
  New Seekers
  (1971)

19 TIE A YELLOW RIBBON ROUND
  THE OLD OAK TREE
  Dawn
  (1973)

20 SAILING
  Rod Stewart
  (1975)

21 UNDER THE MOON OF LOVE
  Showaddywaddy
  (1976)

Showaddywaddy

**22 HIT ME WITH YOUR RHYTHM
STICK**
Ian Dury & The Blockheads
(1978)

23 MISSISSIPPI
Pussycat
(1976)

24 WHEN A CHILD IS BORN (SOLEADO)
Johnny Mathis
(1976)

**25 YOU WON'T FIND ANOTHER
FOOL LIKE ME**
New Seekers
(1974)

26 DON'T GO BREAKING MY HEART
Elton John & Kiki Dee
(1976)

27 WITHOUT YOU
Nilsson
(1972)

28 WELCOME HOME
Peters And Lee
(1973)

29 MY SWEET LORD
George Harrison
(1971)

30 THE NAME OF THE GAME
Abba
(1977)

'Mull of Kintyre', with well over two million sales, is Britain's only double-platinum record and the all-time biggest-selling single within the UK. Significantly, all the top five records on this listing were released within a year of each other in 1977/78, one of the two peak eras for British singles sales (the other being the two years between the end 1963 and the end of '65), when disco, punk and 'Grease' (the film) stimulated every part of the market. Both 'Mull of Kintyre' and 'You're The One That I Want' held the number one slot for 9 consecutive weeks – another remarkable feat in the current 'quick before they vanish' climate of the British charts.

THE THIRTY BIGGEST-SELLING SINGLES OF THE 1970s IN THE USA

Bee Gees

McFadden & Whitehead

1 **YOU LIGHT UP MY LIFE**
   Debby Boone
   (1977)

2 **STAYIN' ALIVE**
   Bee Gees
   (1978)

3 **SHADOW DANCING**
   Andy Gibb
   (1978)

4 **YOU'RE THE ONE THAT I WANT**
   John Travolta & Olivia Newton-John
   (1978)

5 **DISCO LADY**
   Johnnie Taylor
   (1976)

6 **NIGHT FEVER**
   Bee Gees
   (1978)

7 **STAR WARS THEME/CANTINA BAND**
   Meco
   (1977)

8 **HOW DEEP IS YOUR LOVE**
   Bee Gees
   (1977)

9 **LE FREAK**
   Chic
   (1978)

10 **CAR WASH**
   Rose Royce
   (1976)

11 **D'YA THINK I'M SEXY**
   Rod Stewart
   (1978)

12 **YMCA**
   Village People
   (1978)

13 **EMOTION**
   Samantha Sang
   (1978)

14 **DISCO DUCK**
   Rick Dees & His Cast of Idiots
   (1976)

15 **WE ARE THE CHAMPIONS**
   Queen
   (1978)

16 **BOOGIE NIGHTS**
   Heatwave
   (1977)

17 **REUNITED**
   Peaches And Herb
   (1979)

18 **I'LL BE THERE**
   Jackson 5
   (1970)

19 **TRAGEDY**
   Bee Gees
   (1979)

20 **HOT STUFF**
   Donna Summer
   (1979)

21 **LET'S GET IT ON**
   Marvin Gaye
   (1973)

Rose Royce

22 **I WILL SURVIVE**
Gloria Gaynor
(1979)

23 **PLAY THAT FUNKY MUSIC**
Wild Cherry
(1976)

24 **KISS AND SAY GOODBYE**
Manhattans
(1976)

25 **MY SWEET LORD**
George Harrison
(1970)

26 **KILLING ME SOFTLY WITH HIS SONG**
Roberta Flack
(1973)

27 **SHAKE YOUR BODY**
Jacksons
(1979)

28 **AIN'T NO STOPPIN' US NOW**
McFadden & Whitehead
(1979)

29 **PHILADELPHIA FREEDOM**
Elton John Band
(1975)

30 **JOY TO THE WORLD**
Three Dog Night
(1971)

Most of the list above have been reported, or certified by the official American Industry body RIAA, as selling more than two million copies. The bulk of them were released during the last three years of the decade, when record sales were at their highest peak ever in the USA. The biggest American hit of the 1970s, 'You Light Up My Life' by Debby Boone, was number one single for some two-and-a-half months, a feat of longevity at the top unknown since the 1950s. The record barely sold in the UK, while ironically the biggest-selling record in Britain of the 70s, Wings' 'Mull of Kintyre' – which was a chart-topper at exactly the same time – did equally poorly in the USA.

THE ALL-TIME BEST-SELLING SINGLES IN THE U.K. BY GIRL SINGERS

Kate Bush

Cilla Black

1 **ANYONE WHO HAD A HEART**
   Cilla Black
   (1964)

2 **THOSE WERE THE DAYS**
   Mary Hopkin
   (1968)

3 **DON'T CRY FOR ME ARGENTINA**
   Julie Covington
   (1976)

4 **WUTHERING HEIGHTS**
   Kate Bush
   (1978)

5 **ONE DAY AT A TIME**
   Lena Martell
   (1979)

6 **JUST LOVING YOU**
   Anita Harris
   (1978)

7 **MY BOY LOLLIPOP**
   Millie
   (1964)

8 **BOBBY'S GIRL**
   Susan Maughan
   (1962)

9 **YOU'RE MY WORLD**
   Cilla Black
   (1964)

10 **THE WEDDING**
    Julie Rogers
    (1964)

Britain has yet to have a million-selling single by a female soloist, though Cilla Black went more than 90% of the way in 1964, and may well have hit seven figures with 'Anyone Who Had A Heart' through subsequent years, had not the single been deleted for most of the period since. Most of the other entries represent the one outstandingly big hit for each girl concerned; apart from Kate Bush (who has yet to come near repeating the sales of 'Wuthering Heights'), none of these could manage lengthy runs of hits. Much more consistent female chartmakers like Dusty Springfield, Dionne Warwick and Sandie Shaw, on the other hand, failed to have any one hit as big as those above – although Sandie's 1967 Eurovision Song Contests winner 'Puppet On A String' lies fairly close behind Julie Rogers' 'The Wedding', sales-wise.

THE ALL-TIME BEST-SELLING SINGLES IN THE USA BY GIRL SINGERS

Gloria Gaynor

Lulu

1 **YOU LIGHT UP MY LIFE**
Debby Boone
(1977)

2 **HARPER VALLEY P.T.A.**
Jeannie C Riley
(1968)

3 **EMOTION**
Samantha Sang
(1978)

4 **TENNESSEE WALTZ**
Patti Page
(1950)

5 **HOT STUFF**
Donna Summer
(1979)

6 **I WILL SURVIVE**
Gloria Gaynor
(1979)

7 **(HOW MUCH IS THAT)**
DOGGIE IN THE WINDOW?
Patti Page
(1953)

8 **ODE TO BILLIE JOE**
Bobbie Gentry
(1967)

9 **TO SIR WITH LOVE**
Lulu
(1967)

10 **KILLING ME SOFTLY WITH**
HIS SONG
Roberta Flack
(1973)

Although many girl soloists have had million-selling hits in the USA through the years, there have been comparatively few who have taken a title over the two million mark or more, and in fact the list above represents most of them. As with the equivalent UK top ten, most of the songs involved are the one outstandingly large hit from the artist's career, although Donna Summer and Roberta Flack continue to be consistent sellers and could put a second title into a future version of the listing, while Patti Page's two huge sellers from the early 50s mean that after nearly 30 years she is still the only girl so far with two entries.

THE TWENTY WORLDWIDE ALL-TIME BEST-SELLING ALBUMS

Herb Alpert

Carole King

1 **SATURDAY NIGHT FEVER**
Soundtrack
(released 1977)

2 **GREASE**
Soundtrack
(released 1978)

3 **THE SOUND OF MUSIC**
Soundtrack
(released 1965)

4 **SERGEANT PEPPER'S LONELY HEARTS CLUB BAND**
Beatles
(released 1967)

5 **BRIDGE OVER TROUBLED WATER**
Simon & Garfunkel
(released 1970)

6 **THE BEATLES (WHITE DOUBLE ALBUM)**
Beatles
(released 1968)

7 **ABBEY ROAD**
Beatles
(released 1969)

8 **TAPESTRY**
Carole King
(released 1971)

9 **SOUTH PACIFIC**
Soundtrack
(released 1958)

10 **SING WE NOW OF CHRISTMAS (LITTLE DRUMMER BOY)**
Harry Simeone Chorale
(released 1958)

11 **THE DARK SIDE OF THE MOON**
Pink Floyd
(released 1974)

12 **WEST SIDE STORY**
Soundtrack
(released 1961)

13 **RUMOURS**
Fleetwood Mac
(released 1977)

14 **MY FAIR LADY**
Original Broadway Cast
(released 1956)

Stevie Wonder

15 **MARY POPPINS**
   Soundtrack
   (released 1964)

16 **MEET THE BEATLES**
   Beatles
   (released 1964)

17 **THE FIRST FAMILY**
   Vaughn Meader
   (released 1962)

18 **HAIR**
   Original Broadway Cast
   (released 1969)

19 **SONGS IN THE KEY OF LIFE**
   Stevie Wonder
   (released 1976)

20 **WHIPPED CREAM AND**
   OTHER DELIGHTS
   Herb Alpert & the Tijuana Brass
   (released 1956)

This listing is based upon world sales estimates, and there may well be some omissions of later albums for which statistics have not become generally available. In almost every case, the bulk of the sales have been in the USA, still the world's major album market. All those in the top ten have sold more than ten million copies, with 'Saturday Night Fever' estimated as over 30 million. A lot of these albums, particularly the evergreen soundtracks and the items by the Beatles, still sell healthily today many years after their original release.

THE BEST-SELLING ALBUMS OF THE 1950s IN THE UK

South Pac'

1 **SOUTH PACIFIC**
Soundtrack
(released 1958)

2 **MY FAIR LADY**
Original Broadway Cast
(released 1956)

3 **OKLAHOMA**
Soundtrack
(released 1955)

4 **SONGS FOR SWINGING LOVERS**
Frank Sinatra
(released 1956)

5 **WEST SIDE STORY**
Original Broadway Cast
(released 1957)

6 **LONNIE DONEGAN SHOWCASE**
Lonnie Donegan
(released 1956)

7 **COME DANCE WITH ME**
Frank Sinatra
(released 1959)

8 **ELVIS' GOLDEN RECORDS**
Elvis Presley
(released 1958)

9 **MY FAIR LADY**
London Cast
(released 1958)

10 **THE KING AND I**
Soundtrack
(released 1956)

In Britain, albums provided a really tiny part of the sales volume, and the big sellers tended to be those albums – mainly from shows – which had enduring appeal over several years. The UK album charts (a top 10) were first compiled during 1958, and until the end of the decade, only two different titles, 'South Pacific' and Sinatra's 'Come Dance With Me', held the number one position.

THE BEST-SELLING ALBUMS OF THE 1950s IN THE USA

West Side Story

1 **SOUTH PACIFIC**
   Soundtrack
   (released 1958)

2 **MY FAIR LADY**
   Original Broadway Cast
   (released 1956)

3 **TCHAIKOSVKY: PIANO**
   CONCERTO No.1 Van Cliburn
   (released 1958)

4 **RADIO BLOOPERS**
   Kermit Schaeffer
   (released 1953)

5 **JOHNNY'S GREATEST HITS**
   Johnny Mathis
   (released 1958)

6 **SING WE NOW OF CHRISTMAS**
   (LITTLE DRUMMER BOY)
   Harry Simeone Chorale
   (released 1958)

7 **KNOCKERS UP**
   Rusty Warren
   (released 1959)

8 **WEST SIDE STORY**
   Original Broadway Cast
   (released 1957)

9 **HYMNS**
   Tennessee Ernie Ford
   (released 1956)

10 **OKLAHOMA**
   Soundtrack
   (released 1955)

Although the album sales market in America in the 1950s was miniscule compared with its size today, the top ten sellers here were nonetheless all million-plus sellers – although not all of them reached seven figures within the decade of their release, but achieved it over long and consistent sales.

THE BEST-SELLING ALBUMS OF THE 1960s IN THE UK

1 **THE SOUND OF MUSIC**
   Soundtrack
   (released 1965)

2 **WITH THE BEATLES**
   Beatles
   (released 1963)

3 **BEATLES FOR SALE**
   Beatles
   (released 1964)

4 **SERGEANT PEPPER'S LONELY**
   HEARTS CLUB BAND
   Beatles
   (released 1967)

5 **RUBBER SOUL**
   Beatles
   (released 1965)

6 **WEST SIDE STORY**
   Soundtrack
   (released 1961)

7 **THE BEATLES**
   (WHITE DOUBLE ALBUM)
   Beatles
   (released 1968)

8 **REVOLVER**
   Beatles
   (released 1966)

9 **A HARD DAY'S NIGHT**
   Beatles
   (released 1964)

10 **ABBEY ROAD**
    Beatles
    (released 1969)

If this list gives the impression that only one act really sold any albums in Britain during the 1960s, it isn't too far off the mark – at least in terms of really high volume sales. For most UK record buyers, singles were the staple diet, and an album by one of one's favourite acts was an occasional luxury. Only the Beatles had a sufficiently huge and widely-ranging fan following to make each of their albums a premium buy.

The two biggest film soundtracks of the decade – 'The Sound Of Music' and 'West Side Story', scored highly because of their continuing popularity over several years. Both stayed in the upper reaches of the chart while literally hundreds of more ephemeral album sellers came and went, the sales being fuelled continuously by new converts to the films and the music which came from them.

THE BEST-SELLING ALBUMS OF THE 1960s IN THE USA

1 **THE SOUND OF MUSIC**
Soundtrack
(released 1965)

2 **SERGEANT PEPPER'S LONELY HEARTS CLUB BAND**
Beatles
(released 1967)

3 **THE BEATLES (WHITE DOUBLE ALBUM)**
Beatles
(released 1968)

4 **WEST SIDE STORY**
Soundtrack
(released 1961)

5 **MARY POPPINS**
Sountrack
(released 1964)

6 **MEET THE BEATLES**
Beatles
(released 1964)

7 **THE FIRST FAMILY**
Vaughn Meader
(released 1962)

8 **ABBEY ROAD**
Beatles
(released 1969)

9 **HAIR**
Original Broadway Cast
(released 1968)

10 **WHIPPED CREAM AND OTHER DELIGHTS**
Herb Alpert & The Tijuana Brass
(released 1965)

11 **THE MONKEES**
Monkees
(released 1966)

12 **MORE OF THE MONKEES**
Monkees
(released 1967)

13 **JOHN FITZGERALD KENNEDY – A MEMORIAL ALBUM**
(released 1963)

14 **RUBBER SOUL**
Beatles
(released 1965)

15 **BEATLES '65**
Beatles
(released 1964)

16 **MAGICAL MYSTERY TOUR**
Beatles
(released 1967)

17 **LED ZEPPLIN 2**
Led Zeppelin
(released 1967)

18 **IN-A-GADDA-DA-VIDA**
Iron Butterfly
(released 1968)

19 **A HARD DAY'S NIGHT**
Beatles
(released 1964)

20 **S.R.O.**
Herb Alphert & The Tijuana Brass
(released 1966)

The sixties were the first decade of really big album sales in America, and were not unexpectedly dominated by the Beatles, who had several multi-million sellers (which continue to sell today). Soundtracks were still huge, however, as witness the placings of 'The Sound Of Music', 'West Side Story' and 'Mary Poppins'. Vaughn Meader's 'The First Family' was a satirical send-up of the Kennedy family's life at the White House; it was the biggest album success of 1962, selling over five million copies. but had to be quickly deleted just a year later when Kennedy was assassinated. The Kennedy Memorial album, which ironically sold almost as many as the send-up, was a budget-priced set of which all proceeds went to charity.

THE BEST-SELLING ALBUMS OF THE 1970s IN THE UK

Mike Oldfield

1 **BRIDGE OVER TROUBLED WATER**
Simon & Garfunkel
(released 1970)

2 **THE DARK SIDE OF THE MOON**
Pink Floyd
(released 1974)

3 **TUBULAR BELLS**
Mike Oldfield
(released 1973)

4 **20 GOLDEN GREATS**
Beach Boys
(released 1976)

5 **SIMON AND GARFUNKEL'S GREATEST HITS**
Simon & Garfunkel
(released 1974)

6 **ELVIS' 40 GREATEST**
Elvis Presley
(released 1975)

7 **BAND ON THE RUN**
Wings
(released 1974)

8 **20 GOLDEN GREATS**
Shadows
(released 1977)

9 **THE SOUND OF BREAD**
Bread
(released 1976)

10 **20 GOLDEN GREATS**
Diana Ross & The Supremes
(released 1977)

Britain's own Platinum awards for big-selling albums were instituted in the seventies, certification being given to any album achieving £1,000,000 worth of sales at factory-to-dealer level. The British market also became virtually overrun by greatest hits compilations, some from the TV merchandisers (who started the idea off), and even more from the major record companies themselves. The '20 Greatest' of all manner of hit acts graced the number one chart placings (AND secured most of the platinum awards) through the latter half of the decade, though original recordings like Wings' 'Band On The Run' and Mike Oldfield's 'Tubular Bells' did give them a run for their money saleswise.

THE BEST-SELLING ALBUMS OF THE 1970s IN THE USA

Olvia Newton-John and John Travolta from Grease and Saturday Night Fever

1 **SATURDAY NIGHT FEVER**
Soundtrack
(released 1977)

2 **GREASE**
Soundtrack
(released 1978)

3 **BRIDGE OVER TROUBLED WATER**
Simon & Garfunkel
(released 1970)

4 **TAPESTRY**
Carole King
(released 1971)

5 **THE DARK SIDE OF THE MOON**
Pink Floyd
(released 1974)

6 **RUMOURS**
Fleetwood Mac
(released 1977)

7 **SONGS IN THE KEY OF LIFE**
Stevie Wonder
(released 1976)

8 **JESUS CHRIST SUPERSTAR**
Original Studio Cast
(released 1970)

9 **LET IT BE**
Beatles
(released 1970)

10 **HEY JUDE**
Beatles
(released 1970)

Several dozen albums were released in the USA during the seventies to sales of between one and two million, as certified by the RIAA Platinum certifications. Within this large bulk of records it is difficult to establish a meaningful rank order, but the ten titles above have been extracted as having sales well above most of the others. The end of the decade was well and truly dominated by the two gigantic hit soundtracks from 'Saturday Night Fever' and 'Grease' – the two largest-selling albums in record history, while longevity-wise, nothing could match Carole King's 'Tapestry' set, and particularly Pink Floyd's 'The Dark Side Of The Moon', which took up seemingly permanent chart residence.

TEN BEST-SELLING BOOTLEG ALBUMS

1 **GREAT WHITE WONDER**
   (Bob Dylan)

2 **LIV'R THAN YOU'LL EVER BE**
   (Rolling Stones)

3 **YELLOW MATTER CUSTARD**
   (Beatles)

4 **LIVE ON BLUEBERRY HILL**
   (Led Zeppelin)

5 **I WANNA BE A ROCK'N'ROLL STAR**
   (Elvis Presley)

6 **ROYAL ALBERT HALL 1966**
   (Bob Dylan)

7 **BRIGHT LIGHTS, BIG CITY**
   (Rolling Stones)

8 **OMAYYAD**
   (Pink Floyd)

9 **MY GOD**
   (Jethro Tull)

10 **LIVE AT SHEA STADIUM: THE LAST LIVE SHOW**
   (Beatles)

Bootlegs – unauthorised compilations of an artist's work live on stage or from the studio (as opposed to 'pirates', which are simply illegal counterfeit copies of normal releases) – arrived in the rock world in the late 60s, having been around in the jazz, blues and even classical fields for much longer. The first bootleg of note was the Bob Dylan album 'Great White Wonder', featuring then-unissued material from his 'basement tape' sessions with The Band. Although its pressing, distribution and sale were all illegal, the demand for it was such that some estimates put the total sale in various pressings at over a million copies! It is, of course, impossible to verify this, just as it is equally impossible to verify almost anything about bootlegs – where they come from, who got hold of the tapes, who is selling them, etc. What is clear is that 'Great White Wonder' opened a floodgate of sorts, and from the late sixties on virtually any artist or band of any standing at all will have had at least one bootleg made and sold of their work – usually recordings of live concerts, but occasionally more esoteric material.

The listing above is of well-known bootleg releases by some of the most-booted rock names. Dylan, the Beatles, Elvis Presley, the Stones, Pink Floyd, Led Zeppelin, and in more recent years artists like David Bowie, the Sex Pistols, and most notably Bruce Springsteen, have had dozens of bootleg albums released. At the time of writing, they actually seem to be thinner on the ground (in the UK, anyway) than at any time for years. Certainly the authors nor the publishers can help you with regard to any queries about bootleg availability, so please don't write!

THE HIGHEST-PLACED ALBUMS IN THE UK SINGLES CHART

1 **WITH THE BEATLES**
Beatles
(reached 11 in Dec. 1963)

2 **SONGS FOR SWINGING LOVERS**
Frank Sinatra
(reached 12 in Jul. 1956)

3 **A HARD DAY'S NIGHT**
Beatles
(reached 16 in Aug. 1964)

4 **BEATLES FOR SALE**
Beatles
(reached 19 in Jan. 1965)

5 **REVOLVER**
Beatles
(reached 20 in Aug. 1966)

6 **ELVIS IS BACK**
Elvis Presley
(reached 21 in Jul. 1960)

7 **HELP**
Beatles
(reached 22 in Aug. 1965)

8 **SERGEANT PEPPER'S LONELY HEARTS CLUB BAND**
Beatles
(reached 24 in Jun. 1967)

8 **THE BEATLES (WHITE DOUBLE ALBUM)**
Beatles
(reached 24 in Dec. 1968)

10 **G.I. BLUES**
Elvis Presley
(reached 25 in Dec. 1960)

10 **THE ROLLING STONES**
Rolling Stones
(reached 25 in May 1964)

10 **THE ROLLING STONES No.2**
Rolling Stones
(reached 25 in Jan. 1965)

10 **RUBBER SOUL**
Beatles
(reached 25 in Dec. 1965)

As on the face of it this list appears to be a contradiction in terms, some explanation is required. It has been mentioned elsewhere that album sales in the UK were fairly insignificant during the 1950s and much of the 1960s, and although album charts existed, they were measuring a minority section of the market. Therefore, whenever the rare album by a major performer sold in sufficient quantities to place it on a par with singles sales, it was included in the chart with the singles to show a comparison. The listing above includes virtually every title to make the singles top 30 in this way, and it can be seen that the practice persisted into the late 60s, when the Beatles double White Album climbed to number 24. It is significant that only four different acts, all traditionally big sellers of LPs, appear here. Other artists who charted albums in the singles list below number 25 were Lonnie Donegan, Bill Haley & The Comets, and the soundtrack cast of 'Oklahoma'!

109

THE SHADOWS' TEN BEST-SELLING SINGLES (UK)

1 **WONDERFUL LAND**
(1962)
2 **APACHE**
(1960)
3 **DANCE ON**
(1962)
4 **ATLANTIS**
(1963)
5 **FOOT TAPPER**
(1963)
6 **FBI**
(1961)
7 **THE FRIGHTENED CITY**
(1961)
8 **KON-TIKI**
(1961)
9 **THE RISE AND FALL OF FLINGEL BUNT**
(1964)
10 **GUITAR TANGO**
(1962)

From being Cliff Richard's backing group, the Shadows quickly rose to become stars in their own right, and one of the most influential bands of all time, providing the inspiration for scores of thousands of three-guitars-plus-drums outfits all round the world prior to the coming of the Beatles. The Shads had two million-sellers with 'Apache' and 'Wonderful Land', four UK chart toppers, and a couple of dozen top ten hits. They have returned to hit singles prominence in the last two years or so, having only been semi-active on record for much of the seventies.

DUSTY SPRINGFIELD'S TEN BEST-SELLING SINGLES (UK)

1 **YOU DON'T HAVE TO SAY YOU LOVE ME**
(1966)
2 **I ONLY WANT TO BE WITH YOU**
(1963)
3 **I JUST DON'T KNOW WHAT TO DO WITH MYSELF**
(1964)
4 **I CLOSE MY EYES AND COUNT TO TEN**
(1968)
5 **SOME OF YOUR LOVIN'**
(1965)
6 **SON OF A PREACHER MAN**
(1968)
7 **GOING BACK**
(1966)
8 **LOSING YOU**
(1964)
9 **ALL I SEE IS YOU**
(1966)
10 **IN THE MIDDLE OF NOWHERE**
(1965)

Along with Sandie Shaw, Dusty was Britain's most consistent girl hitmaker through the 1960s, and her successful streak only seemed to slow down when she left to live and record in the USA at the end of the decade. 'You Don't Have To Say You Love Me' in 1966 was her biggest seller and a number one hit, but all the titles listed here reached the top ten. Her other really big American success (after 'You Don't...') was 'Wishin' And Hopin' in 1964, not listed here because it was oddly never released as a single in the UK.

Shadows

Dusty Springfield

Frankie Valli

THE FOUR SEASONS' TEN BEST-SELLING SINGLES (USA)

1 **SHERRY** (1962)
2 **BIG GIRLS DON'T CRY** (1962)
3 **RAG DOLL** (1964)
4 **DECEMBER '63 (OH WHAT A NIGHT)** (1975)
5 **WALK LIKE A MAN** (1963)
6 **DAWN (GO AWAY)** (1964)
7 **LET'S HANG ON** (1965)
8 **WHO LOVES YOU** (1975)
9 **CANDY GIRL** (1963)
10 **I'VE GOT YOU UNDER MY SKIN** (1966)

Starting as a gimmick falsetto group on the purposely manufactured single 'Sherry', the Seasons featuring Frankie Valli, settled down as consistent hitmakers for some fifteen years, with eight million-selling singles and six American chart-toppers. At the height of Beatlemania, they still managed to strike back at the top of the charts with 'Dawn' and 'Rag Doll', and when the disco boom arrived in the mid-70s they were well prepared for that too with hustling best-sellers like 'Who Loves You' and 'December '63'.

JERRY LEE LEWIS' TEN BEST-SELLING SINGLES (USA)

1 **WHOLE LOTTA SHAKIN' GOIN' ON**
  (1957)
2 **GREAT BALLS OF FIRE**
  (1957)
3 **BREATHLESS**
  (1958)
4 **HIGH SCHOOL CONFIDENTIAL**
  (1958)
5 **WHAT'D I SAY**
  (1961)
6 **ME AND BOBBY McGHEE**
  (1972)
7 **CHANTILLY LACE**
  (1972)
8 **BREAK UP**
  (1958)
9 **HIGH HEEL SNEAKERS**
  (1964)
10 **WHAT MADE MILWAUKEE FAMOUS**
  (1968)

Jerry Lee Lewis & His Pumping Piano were major stars in the early rock firmament, and one of the genre's most durable and influential acts. The number of bands who have not at some time or another encored or jammed around with 'Whole Lotta Shakin' or 'Great Balls Of Fire' can probably be counted on one hand. Predictably, these were Lewis' best-selling singles, as well as providing his first two international hits. He made a shift to country music during the 1960s and remains within that field to this day, although he still cuts many rock records in his old traditional style. Two of these, 'Me And Bobby McGee' and 'Chantilly Lace' gave him two big comeback pop hits in the USA during 1972.

RICKY NELSON'S TEN BEST-SELLING SINGLES (USA)

1 **POOR LITTLE FOOL**
  (1958)
2 **TRAVELLIN' MAN/HELLO MARY LOU**
  (1961)
3 **NEVER BE ANYONE ELSE BUT YOU/IT'S LATE**
  (1959)
4 **BE-BOP BABY**
  (1957)
5 **LONESOME TOWN**
  (1958)
6 **GARDEN PARTY**
  (1972)
7 **A TEENAGER'S ROMANCE/ I'M WALKIN'**
  (1957)
8 **STOOD UP**
  (1957)
9 **JUST A LITTLE TOO MUCH/ SWEETER THAN YOU**
  (1959)
10 **BELIEVE WHAT YOU SAY**
  (1958)

Getting an excellent start in the record business (he was launched onto disc via his parents' 'Ozzie And Harriett' TV show in the mid-50s), Ricky Nelson developed into probably the most durable, talented and consistently successful of the post-Presley breed of teenage rock idols. All ten titles here were million-sellers, most of them having both sides of the record strongly featured on the chart. 'Garden Party' brought him a big comeback chart hit in the early 1970s, being an autobiographical account of the pitfalls facing the performer on the rock'n'roll revival circuit. He himself has steered largely clear of that circuit in later years, recording in a country rock vein to continued critical acceptance.

Jerry Lee Lewis

Adam Faith

ADAM FAITH'S TEN BEST-SELLING SINGLES (UK)

1 **WHAT DO YOU WANT?**
(1959)
2 **POOR ME**
(1960)
3 **SOMEONE ELSE'S BABY**
(1960)
4 **THE TIME HAS COME**
(1961)
5 **THE FIRST TIME**
(1963)
6 **AS YOU LIKE IT**
(1962)
7 **LONELY PUP**
(1960)
8 **MADE YOU**
(1960)
9 **HOW ABOUT THAT**
(1960)
10 **WHO AM I**
(1961)

Adam Faith crashed onto the British record scene late in 1959 with 'What Do You Want', quickly establishing himself as the major rival to Cliff Richard. His biggest-sellers were mostly in the immediately pre-Beatle years of the sixties, when he scored a whole string of top 10 hits, but he also adapted to the new UK pop sound in 1963 by taking up a backing group (the Roulettes), and cutting 'The First Time', which was one of his biggest hits. He never really penetrated the American market, scoring just one top 30 hit in 1965 with 'It's Alright', oddly enough a track which was only released as a B-side in Britain.

MANFRED MANN'S TEN BEST-SELLING SINGLES (UK)

1 **DO WAH DIDDY DIDDY**
(1964)
2 **THE MIGHTY QUINN**
(1968)
3 **PRETTY FLAMINGO**
(1966)
4 **SEMI-DETACHED SUBURBAN MR JAMES**
(1966)
5 **SHA LA LA**
(1964)
6 **COME TOMORROW**
(1965)
7 **HA HA, SAID THE CLOWN**
(1967)
8 **IF YOU GOTTA GO, GO NOW**
(1965)
9 **FOX ON THE RUN**
(1968)
10 **5-4-3-2-1**
(1964)

The original Manfred Mann (not to be confused with the later Earthband) had a consistent hit streak between 1964 and 1968 which took in the tenures of two lead singers – Paul Jones and Mike D'Abo. Their biggest seller 'Do Wah Diddy Diddy' was also their biggest international hit, but all the ten titles here reached the top 5 in Britain. The group gained a favourable reputation for strong covers of Bob Dylan songs, represented here by 'If You Gotta Go' and 'The Mighty Quinn' (another number one).

BOB DYLAN'S TEN BEST-SELLING SINGLES (USA)

1 **LIKE A ROLLING STONE**
(1965)
2 **RAINY DAY WOMEN NUMBERS 1: AND 35**
(1965)
3 **POSITIVELY 4th STREET**
(1965)
4 **KNOCKIN' ON HEAVEN'S DOOR**
(1973)
5 **LAY LADY LAY**
(1969)
6 **I WANT YOU**
(1966)
7 **SUBTERRANEAN HOMESICK BLUES**
(1965)
8 **JUST LIKE A WOMAN**
(1966)
9 **WIGWAM** (1970)
10 **TONIGHT I'LL BE STAYING HERE WITH YOU**
(1969)

Alongside Lennon & McCartney, Bob Dylan was clearly the most influential force on rock music lyrics from the mid-60s onwards. His major sales market has always been through albums but most of these have in turn spawned a successful single. His biggest singles sellers came during his most overtly pop-oriented phase during 1965/66, bringing million-sellers with 'Like A Rolling Stone', 'Positively 4th Street', and 'Rainy Day Women'. 'Lay Lady Lay' from 1969 was written by invitation for the film 'Midnight Cowboy', but rejected (along with offerings from several other major rock songwriters) in favour of Fred Neil's 'Everybody's Talkin'.

THE MOODY BLUES' TEN BEST-SELLING SINGLES (UK)

1 **NIGHTS IN WHITE SATIN**
(1967)
2 **GO NOW**
(1964)
3 **QUESTION**
(1970)
4 **ISN'T LIFE STRANGE**
(1972)
5 **VOICES IN THE SKY**
(1968)
6 **RIDE MY SEE-SAW**
(1968)
7 **FROM THE BOTTOM OF MY HEART**
(1965)
8 **I'M JUST A SINGER (IN A ROCK AND ROLL BAND)**
(1973)
9 **I DON'T WANT TO GO WITHOUT YOU**
(1965)
10 **BOULEVARD DE LA MADELAINE**
(1966)

Manfred Mann

Bob Dylan

oody Blues

Perhaps better-known as album sellers, the Moodies actually hit the pop scene in late 1964 with the single 'Go Now' which reached number one. 'I Don't Want To Go On Without You' and 'From the Bottom Of My Heart' were the follow-ups, and both reached the top 30. Since then, most of their albums have spawned a hit single of some proportion, although their only other chart-topping hit was with 'Question' in 1970. By far the band's best-selling single (and best-known song), however, is 'Nights In White Satin'. Originally a track from their first smash album 'Days Of Future Passed', it had never completely stopped selling in Britain, and has made the charts three times, the last occasion being in 1979 when it reached the top 10. It also hit number one in the USA in 1972, during its second chart run on that side of the Atlantic.

SIMON AND GARFUNKEL'S TEN BEST-SELLING SINGLES (USA)

1 **BRIDGE OVER TROUBLED WATER**
(1970)
2 **CECILIA**
(1970)
3 **MRS ROBINSON**
(1968)
4 **THE SOUND OF SILENCE**
(1965)
5 **THE BOXER**
(1969)
6 **MY LITTLE TOWN**
(1976)
7 **I AM A ROCK**
(1966)
8 **HOMEWARD BOUND**
(1966)
9 **SCARBOROUGH FAIR/CANTICLE**
(1968)
10 **EL CONDOR PASA**
(1970)

Along with the Everly Brothers probably the best-remembered male due of all time, Paul Simon and Art Garfunkel also managed to do what Don and Phil Everly had not achieved, in continuing to make smash hits individually after splitting up. Their six years together produced one of the most enduring songs ever, 'Bridge Over Troubled Water', as well as three more million-sellers in 'The Sound of Silence', 'Mrs. Robinson' and 'Cecilia'. 'My Little Town' was recorded in the mid-70s as a one-off reunion, and charted in the USA just as if the duo had never been away – alongside their solo recordings.

THE MONKEES' TEN BEST-SELLING SINGLES (USA)

1 **I'M A BELIEVER**
(1966)
2 **DAYDREAM BELIEVER**
(1967)
3 **LAST TRAIN TO CLARKSVILLE**
(1966)
4 **A LITTLE BIT ME, A LITTLE BIT YOU**
(1967)
5 **PLEASANT VALLEY SUNDAY/ WORDS**
(1967)
6 **VALLERI**
(1968)
7 **D.W. WASHBURN**
(1968)
8 **LISTEN TO THE BAND**
(1969)
9 **PORPOISE SONG**
(1968)
10 **TEAR DROP CITY**
(1969)

The Monkees were all the more a staggering phenomenon in the mid-60s for having been a totally 'manufactured' group, put together for the purposes of a TV series. 'I'm A Believer' was a multi-million seller at the end of 1966, and the group had six million-selling singles in all within 18 months, as well as four million-selling albums. Both sides of 'Pleasant Valley Sunday'/'Words' reached the top ten independently, and most of the group's other B-sides were also big chart sellers. Guitarist Mike Nesmith went on to notable solo success in the country-rock field after the Monkees split at the end of the 60s.

on and Garfunkel

CREEDENCE CLEARWATER REVIVAL'S TEN BEST-SELLING SINGLES (USA)

1 **DOWN ON THE CORNER/ FORTUNATE SON**
(1969)
2 **PROUD MARY**
(1969)
3 **BAD MOON RISING**
(1969)
4 **GREEN RIVER**
(1969)
5 **TRAVELLIN' BAND/ WHO'LL STOP THE RAIN**
(1970)
6 **LOOKIN' OUT MY BACK DOOR**
(1970)
7 **SWEET HITCH-HIKER**
(1971)
8 **UP AROUND THE BEND**
(1970)
9 **HAVE YOU EVER SEEN THE RAIN?**
(1971)
10 **SUZIE-Q**
(1968)

The Monkees

eedence Clearwater Revival

With nine million-selling singles in three years, Creedence created a phenomenal niche of chart success for themselves at a time when most bands were concentrating on making and selling albums. 'Bad Moon Rising' was their only chart-topper (on both sides of the Atlantic), but almost all the other singles listed here lined up at number 2 on the chart, generally with the flipsides (notably 'Fortunate Son' and 'Who'll Stop The Rain) not far behind. What's more, despite this singles orientation, they scored two-million selling albums as well.

DAVID ESSEX'S TEN BEST-SELLING SINGLES (UK)

1 **GONNA MAKE YOU A STAR**
(1974)
2 **ROCK ON**
(1973)
3 **HOLD ME CLOSE**
(1975)
4 **OH WHAT A CIRCUS**
(1978)
5 **SILVER DREAM MACHINE**
(1980)
6 **STARDUST**
(1974)
7 **LAMPLIGHT**
(1973)
8 **ROLLIN' STONE**
(1975)
9 **IF I COULD**
(1975)
10 **COOL OUT TONIGHT**
(1977)

SLADE'S TEN BEST-SELLING SINGLES (UK)

1 **MERRY XMAS EVERYBODY**
(1973)
2 **MAMA WEER ALL CRAZY NOW**
(1972)
3 **COME ON FEEL THE NOIZE**
(1973)
4 **COZ I LOVE YOU**
(1971)
5 **TAKE ME BACK 'OME**
(1972)
6 **SKWEEZE PLEEZE ME**
(1973)
7 **LOOK WOT YOU DUN**
(1972)
8 **GUDBUY T'JANE**
(1972)
9 **MY FRIEND STAN**
(1973)
10 **FAR FAR AWAY**
(1974)

Actor-singer David Essex had been making unsuccessful singles for years, before his starrring roles in the films 'That'll Be The Day' and 'Stardust', plus a fruitful liaison with producer Jeff Wayne, suddenly turned him into one of the most consistent British hitmakers of the 1970s. 'Gonna Make You A Star' and 'Hold Me Close' were both number ones, while 'Rock On' (featured in 'That'll Be The Day') reached the top 5 in America as well as being Essex's first major UK hit The later hits 'Oh What A Circus' and 'Silver Dream Machine' came from the show 'Evita' and the film 'Silver Dream Racer' respectively.

Although their crown was challenged by such other teen-stomp bands as Sweet, T Rex and Gary Glitter, Slade ruled British pop music in the early 70s, with ten top 3 hits in little over two years, including several number ones. The biggest of all was 1973's Christmas smash 'Merry Xmas Everybody', which entered the charts at number one, sold a quarter-million in the 48 hours after release, and eventually took the group to their only million-seller. At the end of each year it now returns to shift a few thousand more copies to Christmas partyers. The odd spellings in the titles are deliberate, and represented a Slade trademark.

QUEEN'S TEN BEST-SELLING SINGLES (UK)

1 **BOHEMIAN RHAPSODY**
  (1975)
2 **UNDER PRESSURE**
  (with DAVID BOWIE)
  (1981)
3 **WE ARE THE CHAMPIONS**
  (1977)
4 **CRAZY LITTLE THING**
  CALLED LOVE
  (1979)
5 **KILLER QUEEN**
  (1974)
6 **SOMEBODY TO LOVE**
  (1976)
7 **BICYCLE RACE/**
  FAT-BOTTOMED GIRLS
  (1978)
8 **YOU'RE MY BEST FRIEND**
  (1976)
9 **ANOTHER ONE BITES THE DUST**
  (1980)
10 **SEVEN SEAS OF RHYE**
  (1974)

Slade

Queen

Queen, despite maintaining an unpopular image with much of the rock critic establishment for several years, have nonetheless proved themselves to be one of Britain's most durable big-selling acts of the late 70s and into the 80s. 'Bohemian Rhapsody' was a million-seller on British sales alone, and held the number one position for a staggering nine weeks in 1975, with the group continuing to follow it with at least one major top 5 hit per year ever since, culminating in another number one on the 'Under Pressure' duet with David Bowie, late in 1981.

THE BEST-SELLING TEN SINGLES ON THREE BRITISH RECORD LABELS

COLUMBIA (EMI)

1 **TEARS**
   Ken Dodd
   (1965)

2 **THE CARNIVAL IS OVER**
   Seekers
   (1965)

3 **DIANA**
   Paul Anka
   (1957)

4 **I REMEMBER YOU**
   Frank Ifield
   (1962)

5 **STRANGER ON THE SHORE**
   Mr Acker Bilk
   (1961)

6 **THE YOUNG ONES**
   Cliff Richard
   (1962)

7 **EYE LEVEL**
   Simon Park Orchestra
   (1972)

8 **THE NEXT TIME/BACHELOR BOY**
   Cliff Richard
   (1962)

9 **TWO LITTLE BOYS**
   Rolf Harris
   (1969)

10 **GLAD ALL OVER**
   Dave Clark Five
   (1963)

Before EMI finally launched its own-name label during the early 1970s, Columbia (along with Parlophone) was the company's flagship logo, with most of its biggest-name stars. For many years, Paul Anka's 'Diana' (EMI's biggest-ever selling 10-inch 78rpm single) was the biggest Columbia seller, but the 1960s saw it overtaken by million-sellers by Ken Dodd and the Seekers. The label was largely phased out as the EMI name proper came into use, but has reappeared in the 1980s to handle largely easy-listening music.

DECCA

1 **RELEASE ME**
   Engelbert Humperdinck
   (1967)

2 **GREEN GREEN GRASS OF HOME**
   Tom Jones
   (1966)

3 **THE LAST WALTZ**
   Engelbert Humperdinck
   (1967)

4 **TELSTAR**
   Tornados
   (1962)

5 **THERE GOES MY EVERYTHING**
   Engelbert Humperdinck
   (1967)

6 **THE LAST TIME**
   Rolling Stones
   (1965)

7 **(I CAN'T GET NO) SATISFACTION**
   Rolling Stones
   (1965)

8 **I BELIEVE**
   Bachelors
   (1964)

9 **IT'S NOT UNUSUAL**
   Tom Jones
   (1965)

10 **DIANE**
   Bachelors
   (1964)

One of Britain's oldest major labels, having been launched in the early 1920s, Decca's biggest-selling singles were nevertheless all congregated around the mid-60s, when the label's most consistent acts – Tom Jones, the Rolling Stones, Engelbert Humperdinck and the Bachelors – were all under contract. Apart from the Tornados' 'Telstar', all the records in this list are by these four acts. Decca hit hard times during the 1970s when it lost most of its major artists and the hits were reduced to the occasional one-off novelty. Purchase by the giant Polygram corporation seems to have given it a new lease of chart life into the 1980s, however.

PYE

Dave Clark Five

1 **SAVE YOUR KISSES FOR ME**
Brotherhood Of Man
(1976)

2 **NEEDLES AND PINS**
Searchers
(1964)

3 **WHAT DO YOU WANT TO MAKE THOSE EYES AT ME FOR?**
Emile Ford
(1959)

4 **MY OLD MAN'S A DUSTMAN**
Lonnie Donegan
(1960)

5 **ONE DAY AT A TIME**
Lena Martell
(1979)

6 **HAVE I THE RIGHT**
Honeycombs
(1964)

7 **PUPPET ON A STRING**
Sandie Shaw
(1967)

8 **THIS IS MY SONG**
Petula Clark
(1967)

9 **MATCHSTALK MEN AND MATCHSTALK CATS AND DOGS**
Bryan & Michael
(1978)

10 **ANGELO**
Brotherhood of Man

The Bachelors

The Honeycombs

Pye was Britain's major source of hit singles through the 1950s and 1960s after the giant EMI and Decca companies. Beginning as Polygon and then Nixa Records before leasing its best known trade name from Pye Electronics of Cambridge (the lease has now expired, and the label has become PRT records), Pye had a hit roster to rival the majors for several years, the most consistent act apart from those represented in this top ten sellers chart being the Kinks, who scored some two dozen chart hits in the UK.

THE ALL-TIME BEST-SELLING INSTRUMENTAL SINGLES IN BRITAIN

MR. ACKER BILK AND HIS PARAMOUNT JAZZ BAND

1 **STRANGER ON THE SHORE**
   Mr Acker Bilk
   (1961)

2 **EYE LEVEL**
   Simon Park Orchestra
   (1972)

3 **TELSTAR**
   Tornados
   (1962)

4 **AMAZING GRACE**
   Royal Scots Dragoons Guards Band
   (1972)

5 **WONDERFUL LAND**
   Shadows
   (1962)

6 **APACHE**
   Shadows
   (1960)

7 **CHI MAI**
   Ennio Morricone
   (1981)

8 **MOULDY OLD DOUGH**
   Lieutenant Pigeon
   (1972)

9 **THE GOOD, THE BAD AND THE UGLY**
   Hugo Montenegro
   (1968)

10 **DANCE ON**
   Shadows
   (1962)

'Stranger On The Shore' and 'Eye Level' are the only two non-vocals ever to have sold more than a million copies in Britain. Interestingly, both were TV themes; 'Stranger' from a 1961 series of the same title, and 'Eye Level' from the 'Van Der Valk' series of the early 1970s. Ennio Morricone's 'Chi Mai', with some 600,000 sales by far the biggest instrumental of recent years, was also used on TV as the theme for two series – 'An Englishman's Castle' in 1971 and 'The Life And Times Of Lloyd George' in 1981 – the latter appearance turning it into a smash hit. Morricone also wrote the film theme 'The Good, The Bad And The Ugly', but although he had a number 2 album seller with it in 1969, it was the cover version of the theme by Hugo Montenegro which went to the top in Britain and number 2 in the USA during 1968.

'Telstar' by the Tornados was the UK's all-time best-selling instrumental disc on a worldwide basis, reaching number one in almost every country which published a chart. It has remained on catalogue in Britain ever since 1962, edging its way ever nearer to the domestic million sale which is at present only a few thousand copies off. At one time, the Tornados were hailed as major opposition to the Shadows, but in the event they fell some 25 short of the latter group's 30-odd chart hits. Fittingly, the Shadows themselves are the most-placed act in this top ten, with three of their four chart-toppers of the early 1960s.

THE ALL-TIME BEST SELLING INSTRUMENTAL SINGLES IN THE USA

Tornadoes

1 **LOVE IS BLUE**
   Paul Mauriat
   (1967)

2 **STAR WARS THEME/CANTINA BAND**
   Meco
   (1977)

3 **THEME FROM 'A SUMMER PLACE'**
   Percy Faith
   (1960)

4 **THE HARRY LIME THEME (THE THIRD MAN)**
   Anton Karas
   (1950)

5 **CHERRY PINK AND APPLE BLOSSOM WHITE**
   Perez Prado
   (1955)

6 **LOVE THEME FROM 'ROMEO & JULIET'**
   Henry Mancini
   (1969)

7 **TELSTAR**
   Tornados
   (1962)

8 **SAIL ALONG SILVERY MOON**
   Billy Vaughn
   (1957)

9 **A FIFTH OF BEETHOVEN**
   Walter Murphy
   (1976)

10 **THEME FROM 'ROCKY' (GONNA FLY NOW)**
   Bill Conti
   (1977)

Most of America's really big-selling non-vocal records through the years have been orchestral items or film themes, or both. Rock instrumentals always had it harder than in Britain where there were bands like the Shadows to set the trend. This puts 'Telstar' rather out on its own in this list, although 'Cherry Pink' and 'Sail Along' were big dance tunes in their day too, and the disco instrumental smashes by Walter Murphy and Meco have continued this tradition.

THE HIGHEST-PLACED B-SIDES TO CHART INDEPENDENTLY IN THE UK SINGLES CHART

Sammy Davis Jr.

1 **ROCK-A-HULA BABY**
Elvis Presley
(reached 3 in 1962.A-side **CAN'T HELP FALLING IN LOVE** reached 1)

1 **BACHELOR BOY**
Cliff Richard
(reached 3 in 1963. A-side **THE NEXT TIME** reached 1)

3 **THE GIRL OF MY BEST FRIEND**
Elvis Presley
(reached 5 in 1960. A-side **A MESS OF BLUES** reached 3)

4 **LET ME GO LOVER**
Dean Martin
(reached 5 in 1955. A-side **THE NAUGHTY LADY OF SHADY LANE** reached 4)

5 **IT'S TOO SOON TO KNOW**
Pat Boone
(reached 8 in 1958. A-side **A WONDERFUL TIME UP THERE** reached 2)

6 **MAMA**
Connie Francis
(reached 8 in 1960. A-side **ROBO MAN** reached 3)

7 **ONLY YOU**
Platters
(reached 8 in 1956. A-side **THE GREAT PRETENDER** reached 6)

8 **LET ME GO LOVER**
Ruby Murray
(reached 8 in 1955. A-side **HAPPY DAYS AND LONELY NIGHTS** reached 7)

9 **DO YOU WANT TO DANCE?**
Cliff Richard
(reached 9 in 1962. A-side **I'M LOOKING OUT THE WINDOW** reached 2)

10 **THE STRANGER**
Shadows
(reached 10 in 1960. A-side **MAN OF MYSTERY** reached 6)

11 **EVIL HEARTED YOU**
Yardbirds
(reached 10 in 1965. A-side **STILL I'M SAD** reached 9)

12 **CATCH A FALLING STAR**
Perry Como
(reached 11 in 1958. A-side **MAGIC MOMENTS** reached 1)

The Platters

12 SHE TAUGHT ME HOW TO YODEL
Frank Ifield
(reached 11 in 1962. A-side
LOVESICK BLUES reached 1)

14 HERNANDO'S HIDEAWAY
Johnnie Ray
(reached 11 in 1955. A-side **HEY
THERE** reached 5)

**14 WHEN JOHNNY COMES
MARCHING HOME**
Adam Faith
(reached 11 in 1960. A-side **MADE
YOU** reached 5)

16 YOU DON'T OWE ME A THING
Johnnie Ray
(reached 11 in 1957. A-side **LOOK
HOMEWARD ANGEL** reached 7)

17 SOMETHING'S GOTTA GIVE
Sammy Davis Jr
(reached 11 in 1955. A-side **LOVE
ME OR LEAVE ME** reached 9)

18 YOU MY LOVE
Frank Sinatra
(reached 12 in 1953. A-side **THREE
COINS IN THE
FOUNTAIN** reached 1)

19 MAMA
David Whitfield
(reached 12 in 1955. A-side
EV'RYWHERE reached 4)

20 DEAD OR ALIVE
Lonnie Donegan
(reached 12 in 1956. A-side **BRING
A LITTLE WATER SILVIE**
reached 8)

A holdover from the days when sheet music sold more than records, and people went into record shops to ask for songs rather than artists, was the practice of charting both sides of a single independently when the B-side was securing a respectable percentage of the sales. The Beatles probably killed the procedure in Britain (everybody just asked for "the new Beatles", so while some people wanted one title and others a different one, chart return dealers couldn't distinguish and totalled the lot up), and by the end of the sixties it was almost dead in the USA too. Some B-sides sold incredibly well during the 50s and 60s, however, as this listing demonstrates.

THE HIGHEST-PLACED EPs IN THE UK SINGLES CHART

1 **MAGICAL MYSTERY TOUR (DOUBLE EP)**
Beatles
(1 in Jan. 1968)

1 **THE ROUSSOS PHENOMENON**
Demis Roussos
(1 in Jul. 1976)

1 **TOO MUCH TOO YOUNG: SPECIALS AKA LIVE**
Specials
(1 in Feb. 1980)

4 **ALL-STAR HIT PARADE**
Various
(2 in Jul. 1956)

5 **TWIST AND SHOUT**
Beatles
(3 in Aug. 1963)

6 **FOUR FROM TOYAH**
Toyah
(4 in Mar. 1981)

7 **GOT LIVE IF YOU WANT IT**
Rolling Stones
(6 in Jul. 1965)

8 **THE ONE IN THE MIDDLE**
Manfred Mann
(7 in Jul. 1965)

8 **THE GOLDEN YEARS**
Motorhead
(7 in May 1981)

10 **EXTENDED PLAY**
Bryan Ferry
(8 in Sept. 1976)

11 **GRANDMA'S PARTY**
Paul Nicholas
(9 in Jan. 1977)

12 **EXPRESSO BONGO**
Cliff Richard
(11 in Feb. 1960)

13 **LONG TALL SALLY**
Beatles
(12 in Jul. 1964)

13 **FOLLOW THAT DREAM**
Elvis Presley
(12 in Jul. 1962)

13 **ALL MY LOVING**
Beatles
(12 in Feb. 1964)

13 **FIVE BY FIVE**
Rolling Stones
(12 in Sept. 1964)

13 **IDOL ON PARADE**
Anthony Newley
(13 in May 1959)

17 **AIN'T GONNA KISS YA**
Searchers
(13 in Oct. 1963)

17 **THE UNIVERSAL SOLDIER**
Donovan
(13 in Sept. 1965)

20 **JAILHOUSE ROCK**
Elvis Presley
(15 in Feb. 1958)

20 **SPOT THE PIGEON**
Genesis
(15 in Jun. 1977)

EPs – basically 4-track 7″ releases selling for the price of about $1\frac{1}{2}$ singles – were a familiar fixture in the 1950s and the early 60s in Britain, although the format has never meant nearly so much in the USA. They were virtually killed off in the UK during the later 60s by the advent of budget albums, but then re-emerged in the mid-70s as a sort of deluxe single , sometimes selling at just single price (though not always) and mostly resurrecting the old 4-track format. Three EPs have actually topped the singles chart, two of them within the last five years; the Beatles earlier success with 'Magical Mystery Tour' was all the more remarkable for the release being a double EP with eight tracks (and a much higher price tag.)

JAZZ RECORDINGS WHICH WERE BIG POP HITS

TAKE FIVE
Dave Brubeck
(1961)
WALK ON THE WILD SIDE
Jimmy Smith
(1962)
DESAFINADO
Stan Getz and Charlie Byrd
(1963)
THE 'IN' CROWD
Ramsey Lewis Trio
(1965)
FEELS SO GOOD
Chuck Mangione
(1968)
I'VE GOT A WOMAN
Jimmy McGriff
(1962)
ALSO SPRACH ZARATHUSTRA
(2001)
Deodato
(1973)
EXPERIMENTS WITH MICE
Johnny Dankworth
(1956)
MISTY
Richard 'Groove' Holmes
(1966)
TOPSY
Cozy Cole
(1958)

THE TEN MOST SUCCESSFUL SURFING RECORDS IN THE USA

1 **WIPE OUT**
  Surfaris
  (4 in Aug. 1963 and 11 in Oct. 1966)
2 **SURF CITY**
  Jan And Dean
  (1 in Jul. 1963)
3 **SURFIN' USA**
  Beach Boys
  (3 in May 1963)
4 **PIPELINE**
  Chantays
  (4 in May 1963)
5 **SURFER GIRL**
  Beach Boys
  (5 in Sept. 1963)
6 **SURFIN' BIRD**
  Trashmen
  (4 in Jan. 1964)
7 **SURFIN' SAFARI**
  Beach Boys
  (12 in Oct. 1962)
8 **RIDE THE WILD SURF**
  Jan And Dean
  (16 in Oct. 1964)
9 **PENETRATION**
  Pyramids
  (17 in Mar. 1964)
10 **SURFER'S STOMP**
  Mar-Kets
  (31 in Feb. 1962)

This ignores the British trad jazz boom of the early 60's and also the recent growth of jazz funk fusion which has thrown up many chart hits in the disco field:

Perhaps because of its close associations with the sport and the climate, the bulk of the surf music craze was restricted to California. Many of the hundreds of vocal and (especially) instrumental records made in the genre only sold within – and often were only distributed within – California.

Nonetheless, the ten above were the biggest of the two dozen or so which broke nationally. Numbers 1,4,9 and 10 are instrumentals, and the Pyramids are now more remembered for all having totally bald heads than for their top 20 hit 'Penetration'.

Jimmy Smith

TEN HIT SONGS FROM CLASSICAL PIECES

Barry Manilow

AN AMERICAN TUNE
Paul Simon
(Johann Sebastian Bach – O SACRED HEAD from the ST. MATTHEW PASSION)

HELLO MUDDAH, HELLO FADDAH
Allan Sherman
(Poncielli – DANCE OF THE HOURS)

NIGHT
Jackie Wilson
(Saint-Sans – MY HEART AT THY SWEET VOICE from SAMSON AND DELILAH

COULD IT BE MAGIC
Barry Manilow
(Chopin – PRELUDE IN C MINOR)

ALL BY MYSELF
Eric Carmen
(Rachmaninov – PIANO CONCERTO NO.2)

ASIA MINOR
Kokomo
(Greig – PIANO CONCERTO NO. 1)

BUMBLE BOOGIE
B. Bumble & The Stingers
(Rimsky-Korsakov – FLIGHT OF THE BUMBLE BEE)

SMOKEY BLUE'S AWAY
A New Generation
(Dvorak – THE 'NEW WORLD' SYMPHONY)

A LOVER'S CONCERTO
Toys
(Johann Sebastian Bach – MINUET IN G)

ALONE AT LAST
Jackie Wilson
(Tchaikovsky – PIANO CONCERTO NO.1 IN B-FLAT MINOR)

Melodic sections of the classics have always provided fair pickings for pop songwriting. The results have occasionally caused bannings by broadcasting organizations (notably the BBC) which found them in 'bad taste', and also (but more rarely) occasional objections from composers' estates. Those listed above overcame such drawbacks to become big chart hits (although Jackie Wilson's 'Night' was banned in Britain for copyright reasons), and there have been many other successful classical adaptations from artists as diverse as the Four Seasns, Vince Hill, Donald Peers, Duane Eddy, the Beach Boys, and the (in)famous 'Saturday Night At The Duck Pond' ('Swan Lake' to you) by UK band the Cougars. Elvis Presley even recorded the same basic songs in versions with slightly different lyrics to TWO different classical melodies – 'Tonight's Alright For Love' (Strauss') 'Tales From The Vienna Woods') and 'Tonight Is So Right For Love' (Offenbach's 'La Barcarolle' from 'Tales Of Hoffman').

128

TEN HITS IN THE UK SUNG IN A FOREIGN LANGUAGE

Fairport Convention

1 **VOLARE (NEL BLU DIPINTO DI BLU)**
Domenico Modugno
(11 in 1958 – ITALIAN)

2 **MORGEN**
Ivor Robic
(28 in 1959 – GERMAN)

3 **YA YA TWIST**
Petula Clark
(12 in 1962 – FRENCH)

4 **SUKIYAKI**
Kyu Sakamoto
(9 in 1963 – JAPANESE)

5 **DOMINIQUE**
The Singing Nun
(4 in 1963 – FRENCH)

6 **NON HO L'ETA PER AMARTI**
Gigliola Cinquetti
(16 in 1964 – ITALIAN)

7 **TOUS LES GARCONS ET LES FILLES**
Francoise Hardy
(36 in 1964 – FRENCH)

8 **SI TU DOIS PARTIR**
Fairport Convention
(21 in 1969 – FRENCH)

9 **A-BA-NI-BI**
Izhar Cohen & The Alpha-Beta
(20 in 1978 – ISRAELI)

10 **BEGIN THE BEGUINE**
Julio Iglesias
(in 1981 – SPANISH)

The English-speaking (and singing) world is remarkably reticent with regard to songs sung in other languages; by and large nobody wants to know. The list above does not show every foreign-language recording to have made the British charts, but if features at least 50 per cent of them, which in nearly thirty years hardly represents the best of batting odds for non-English lyrics. English-language versions of 'Volare', 'Morgen' ('One More Sunrise') and 'Si Tu Dois Partir' ('If You Gotta Go, Go Now') scored significantly better in the charts than their foreign-language equivalents noted here.

129

SECTION 3

POT POURRI

THE TEN SINGLES WITH THE LONGEST DURATION AT NUMBER ONE (UK)

Slim Whitman

1 **I BELIEVE**
Frankie Laine
(1953 – top for 18 weeks)

2 **ROSE MARIE**
Slim Whitman
(1955 – top for 10 weeks)

2 **CARA MIA**
David Whitfield
(1954 – top for 10 weeks)

4 **SECRET LOVE**
Doris Day
(1954 – top for 9 weeks)

4 **OH MEIN PAPA**
Eddie Calvert
(1954 – top for 9 weeks)

4 **IT'S NOW OR NEVER**
Elvis Presley
(1960 – top for 9 weeks)

4 **DIANA**
Paul Anka
(1957 – top for 9 weeks)

4 **MULL OF KINTYRE**
Wings
(1977 – top for 9 weeks)

4 **BOHEMIAN RHAPSODY**
Queen
(1975 – top for 9 weeks)

4 **YOU'RE THE ONE THAT I WANT**
John Travolta &
Olivia Newton-John
(1978 – top for 9 weeks)

Just ten records have topped the singles chart for nine weeks or more in Britain. 'I Believe' didn't achieve quite all of its staggering 18-week run in one go – after 16 straight weeks at the top (still well clear of everything else), it stepped down to allow Mantovani's 'Theme From Moulin Rouge' a two-week run. That done, 'I Believe' returned to the top for a further fortnight by way of an encore.

Records which topped the chart for eight weeks included the Everly Brothers' 'Cathy's Clown' and 'All I Have To Do Is Dream'; 'The Young Ones' from Cliff Richard; Al Martino's 'Here In My Heart'; and 'Wonderful Land' by the Shadows.

132

THE TEN SINGLES WITH THE LONGEST DURATION AT NUMBER ONE (USA – FROM 1950 ONWARDS)

Debby Boone

1 **GOODNIGHT IRENE**
   Weavers
   (1950 – top for 13 weeks)

2 **THE HARRY LIME THEME**
   (THE THIRD MAN)
   Anton Karas
   (1950 – top for 11 weeks)

2 **CRY**
   Johnnie Ray
   (1951 – top for 11 weeks)

2 **VAYA CON DIOS**
   Les Paul & Mary Ford
   (1953 – top for 11 weeks)

2 **DON'T BE CRUEL**
   Elvis Presley
   (1956 – top for 11 weeks)

2 **YOU LIGHT UP MY LIFE**
   Debby Boone
   (1977 – top for 11 weeks)

7 **SONG FROM MOULIN ROUGE**
   Percy Faith Orchestra
   (1953 – top for 10 weeks)

7 **CHERRY PINK AND APPLE**
   BLOSSOM WHITE
   Perez Prado
   (1955 – top for 10 weeks)

7 **MACK THE KNIFE**
   Bobby Darin
   (1959 – top for 10 weeks)

7 **TENNESSEE WALTZ**
   Patti Page
   (1950 – top for 10 weeks)

Prior to 1950, during the first decade of American singles charts, a three-month stay at number one was almost par for the course, which is why we've taken this listing from 1950 – to avoid filling it with records from 1940 and 1941. Thirteen weeks at the top is in fact the all-time longest run; records in the forties which equalled the Weavers' achievement were 'Frenesi' by Artie Shaw and 'I've Heard That Song Before' by Harry James.

133

THE TEN ALBUMS WITH THE LONGEST DURATION AT NUMBER ONE (UK) – FROM 1959

The Sound of Music

1 **SOUTH PACIFIC**
   Soundtrack
   (83 weeks, 1959 – 1961)

2 **THE SOUND OF MUSIC**
   Soundtrack
   (68 weeks, 1965 – 1968)

3 **PLEASE PLEASE ME**
   Beatles
   (30 weeks, 1963)

4 **SERGEANT PEPPER'S LONELY HEARTS CLUB BAND**
   Beatles
   (27 weeks, 1967 – 1968)

5 **BRIDGE OVER TROUBLED WATER**
   Simon & Garfunkel
   (26 weeks, 1970 – 1971)

6 **G.I. BLUES**
   Elvis Presley
   (25 weeks, 1960)

7 **WITH THE BEATLES**
   Beatles
   (21 weeks, 1963-1964)

7 **A HARD DAY'S NIGHT**
   Beatles
   (21 weeks, 1964)

9 **BLUE HAWAII**
   Elvis Presley
   (19 weeks, 1962)

10 **ABBEY ROAD**
    Beatles
    (18 weeks, 1969 – 1970)

The album market in Britain nowadays moves rapidly, with four or five weeks at the top being a long residence for any album. During the 1960s, things were considerably more stable, with steady, long-period sellers the order of the day. Hardly any of these albums scored their chart-topping total of weeks all in one go, however – the Beatles' 'Please Please Me' is a notable exception.

THE TEN ALBUMS WITH THE LONGEST DURATION AT NUMBER ONE (USA)

Mick Fleetwood, Christine McVie and John McVie of Fleetwood Mac

1 **SOUTH PACIFIC**
   Original Cast
   (69 weeks, 1949 – 1950)

2 **WEST SIDE STORY**
   Soundtrack
   (54 weeks, 1962 – 1963)

2 **SOUTH PACIFIC**
   Soundtrack
   (54 weeks, 1958 – 1959)

4 **SWITCHED ON BACH**
   Walter Carlos & Benjamin
   Folkman
   (40 weeks, 1968 – 70)

5 **THE STUDENT PRINCE**
   Mario Lanza
   (36 weeks, 1954)

6 **CALYPSO**
   Harry Belafonte
   (31 weeks, 1956)

7 **RUMOURS**
   Fleetwood Mac
   (30 weeks, 1978)

8 **HAIR**
   Original Broadway Cast
   (20 weeks, 1969)

8 **BLUE HAWAII**
   Elvis Presley
   (20 weeks, 1961)

10 **SERGEANT PEPPER'S LONELY**
   HEARTS CLUB BAND
   Beatles
   (19 weeks, 1967)

The real cases of album longevity inevitably occurred in the early, slow and steady period of the American LP charts, but there have been long stays more recently, notably those of Carlos/Folkman at the start of the seventies, and of Fleetwood Mac with 'Rumours' towards the end. The pattern of album sales is still steadier today in the States than the rapid up-and-down UK album chart activity, but nonetheless Mac's 30-week feat is not likely to be repeated again in the present climate.

THE TEN SINGLES WITH THE LONGEST DURATION IN THE BRITISH CHARTS

Frank Sinatra

1 **MY WAY**
Frank Sinatra
(127 weeks from 1970)

2 **AMAZING GRACE**
Judy Collins
(70 weeks from 1970)

3 **ROCK AROUND THE CLOCK**
Bill Haley & The Comets
(60 weeks from 1955)

4 **RELEASE ME**
Englebert Humperdinck
(57 weeks from 1967)

5 **STRANGER ON THE SHORE**
Mr Acker Bilk
(55 weeks from 1961)

6 **I LOVE YOU BECAUSE**
Jim Reeves
(48 weeks from 1964)

7 **LET'S TWIST AGAIN**
Chubby Checker
(47 weeks from 1961)

8 **DECK OF CARDS**
Wink Martindale
(41 weeks from 1959)

9 **RIVERS OF BABYLON/**
BROWN GIRL IN THE RING
Boney M
(40 weeks from 1978)

9 **TIE A YELLOW RIBBON ROUND**
THE OLD OAK TREE
Dawn
(40 weeks from 1973)

Considering the short chart life of the average single in Britain (about 3 months for a good number one hit), there are some staggering feats of longevity here. However, these are cumulative totals, and the top three records all scored from a number of re-entries into the chart as their popularity asserted itself once again. This is particularly true of 'Rock Around The Clock', which has had umpteen different chart runs from 1955 through to 1974. The records by Englebert Humperdinck, Acker Bilk, Jim Reeves, Boney M and Dawn did, however, score their full quota of charts weeks in one continuous run.

136

THE TEN SINGLES WITH THE LONGEST DURATION IN THE AMERICAN CHARTS

Chubby Checker

1 **WHITE CHRISTMAS**
Bing Crosby
(72 weeks)

2 **I GO CRAZY**
Paul Davis
(40 weeks)

3 **WONDERFUL, WONDERFUL**
Johnny Mathis
(39 weeks)

3 **THE TWIST**
Chubby Checker
(39 weeks)

5 **BLUE TANGO**
Leroy Anderson
(38 weeks)

5 **SO RARE**
Jimmy Dorsey
(38 weeks)

5 **WHY ME?**
Kris Kristofferson
(38 weeks)

8 **THE WAYWARD WIND**
Gogi Grant
(37 weeks)

9 **LOVE LETTERS IN THE SAND**
Pat Boone
(34 weeks)

9 **BE MY LOVE**
Mario Lanza
(34 weeks)

9 **IT'S NOT FOR ME TO SAY**
Johnny Mathis
(34 weeks)

'White Christmas's' 72 weeks on the chart were spread over more than 20 years in much shorter segments, as the record picked up sales again with each succeeding Christmas, and thus re-charted. No one continuous run by the record approaches those of any of the other discs on this list. Chubby Checker's 'The Twist' also had two completely independent runs in 1960 and 1962, reaching number one in each case and charting for 18 and 21 weeks respectively. Paul Davis' 'I Go Crazy' from 1977 holds the all-time record for continuous chart action with its run of 40 weeks, finally beating by one week the record which Johnny Mathis' 'Wonderful, Wonderful' had held for ten years.

THE TEN ALBUMS WITH THE LONGEST DURATION IN THE BRITISH CHARTS

Pink F

1 **THE SOUND OF MUSIC**
Soundtrack
(362 weeks from 1965)

2 **SOUTH PACIFIC**
Soundtrack
(306 weeks from 1958)

3 **BRIDGE OVER TROUBLED WATER**
Simon And Garfunkel
(285 weeks from 1970)

4 **GREATEST HITS**
Simon And Garfunkel
(179 weeks from 1972)

5 **WEST SIDE STORY**
Soundtrack
(153 weeks from 1962)

6 **THE DARK SIDE OF THE MOON**
Pink Floyd
(140 weeks from 1974)

7 **THE BLACK AND WHITE MINSTREL SHOW**
George Mitchell Minstrels
(124 weeks from 1960)

8 **TUBULAR BELLS**
Mike Oldfield
(123 weeks from 1973)

9 **BEST OF THE BEACH BOYS, VOL.1**
Beach Boys
(120 weeks from 1966)

10 **LED ZEPPELIN II**
Led Zeppelin
(118 weeks from 1969)

The British album charts, which started some ten years after their American counterparts, and consisted of only short listings (a top 10 or 20) until the late 1960s, obviously miss some of the long stayers from earlier years. They in fact tell a different story altogether, with only one title – 'Dark Side Of The Moon' – to be found in both listings. The top two UK albums, the soundtracks of 'The Sound Of Music' and 'South Pacific' are just outside the American top ten.

THE TEN ALBUMS WITH THE LONGEST DURATION IN THE AMERICAN CHARTS

Johnny Mathis

1 **JOHNNY'S GREATEST HITS**
Johnny Mathis
(490 weeks from 1958)

2 **MY FAIR LADY**
Original Cast
(482 weeks from 1956)

3 **SOUTH PACIFIC**
Original Cast
(427 weeks from 1949)

4 **THE DARK SIDE OF THE MOON**
Pink Floyd
(400 weeks from 1974)

5 **MY FAVORITE CHOPIN**
Van Cliburn
(360 weeks from 1966)

6 **SWITCHED ON BACH**
**Walter Carlos & Benjamin
Folkman**
(310 weeks from 1968)

7 **TAPESTRY**
Carole King
(302 weeks from 1971)

8 **TCHAIKOVSKY: PIANO
CONCERTO No.1**
Van Cliburn
(297 weeks from 1958)

9 **THE SOUND OF MUSIC**
Original Cast
(277 weeks from 1959)

10 **2001: A SPACE ODYSSEY**
Soundtrack
(271 weeks from 1968)

There are a select breed of albums which seem to have almost eternal appeal, as indicated by the longevity records above – Johnny Mathis' album at the top of the list stayed on the chart for 9½ years! Rock albums can be expected to have a more ephemeral sales life than easy listening, show or classical music, which makes it all the more remarkable that Pink Floyd should be at number 4 with 'The Dark Side Of The Moon'. This is still on the album chart as this book is being written, having just hit 400 weeks in the latest chart to hand. Admittedly it has to stay around for the best part of two more years to become all time champion, but its sales show no sign of flagging yet.

TEN BRITISH NUMBER ONE ONE-HIT WONDERS

Anita Ward

1 **IT'S ALMOST TOMORROW**
   Dream Weavers
   (1956)
2 **WHEN**
   Kalin Twins
   (1958)
3 **TELL LAURA I LOVE HER**
   Ricky Valance
   (1960)
4 **MICHELLE**
   Overlanders
   (1966)
5 **IN THE YEAR 2525**
   (EXORDIUM AND TERMINUS)
   Zager And Evans
   (1969)
6 **SPIRIT IN THE SKY**
   Norman Greenbaum
   (1970)
7 **GRANDAD**
   Clive Dunn
   (1971)
8 **NO CHARGE**
   J.J. Barrie
   (1976)

9 **MATCHSTALK MEN AND**
   MATCHSTALK
   CATS AND DOGS
   Brian & Michael
   (1978)
10 **RING MY BELL**
   Anita Ward
   (1979)

Britain too has had a small select bunch of hitmakers with nought but a number one hit to their credit. Zager And Evans must take some sort of award here, as they and 'In The Year 2525' appear on the American list as well. Again, a lot of these hits could be described as novelties, though it is perhaps difficult to see why commercial teen-appeal acts of their day like Ricky Valance and the Overlanders failed to follow their chart-toppers with at least SOME modicum of sales action. One piece of irony: although Brian and Michael called it a day success-wise after 'Matchstalk Men', the backup singers on that record, St. Winifred's School Choir, DID score another hit later on in their own right, with 'There's No-One Quite Like Grandma', which reached number 2 in 1980.

TEN AMERICAN NUMBER ONE ONE-HIT WONDERS

1 **PISTOL PACKIN' MAMA**
   Al Dexter
   (1943)

2 **THE HARRY LIME THEME**
   (THE THIRD MAN)
   Anton Karas
   (1950)

3 **IT'S IN THE BOOK**
   Johnny Standley
   (1952)

4 **I SAW MOMMY KISSING**
   SANTA CLAUS
   Jimmy Boyd
   (1952)

5 **LET ME GO LOVER**
   Joan Weber
   (1955)

6 **GET A JOB**
   Silhouettes
   (1958)

7 **LITTLE STAR**
   Elegants
   (1958)

8 **ALLEY-OOP**
   Hollywood Argyles
   (1960)

9 **DOMINIQUE**
   Singing Nun
   (1963)

10 **IN THE YEAR 2525**
   (EXORDIUM AND TERMINUS)
   Zager And Evans
   (1969)

One-hit wonders have always been a regular feature of the popular singles charts and most certainly always will be. Much rarer, though, is the case of an act whose only chartmaker is a number one hit. Under normal circumstances, the sheer momentum of the exposure brought about by a chart-topping record will be enough to pre-sell its follow-up into some sort of chart position – even though it be a lowly placing for a couple of weeks until the public decides that it really doesn't want any more of the same after all. The follow-ups to the ten records above, however, failed to find any purchase in the top 100 despite that initial number one presence (or in the top 30 as far as the earliest four titles are concerned, as the longer chart was not existence then). Generally, this says something about the decided NON-impact of the acts themselves, as opposed to their number one records, which were almost all novelties of one kind or another. The Hollywood Argyles maybe have the excuse that they never really existed at all, and did find later success anyway via individual members like Sandy Nelson. As for the rest of them, your guess is as good as ours.

TEN BRITISH ONE-HIT WONDERS IN THE USA

Roger Whittaker

1 **CHARLIE DRAKE**
   (with **MY BOOMERANG WON'T COME BACK** in 1962)

2 **DAVID AND JONATHAN**
   (with **MICHELLE** in 1966)

3 **PIPKINS**
   (with **GIMME DAT DING** in 1970)

4 **C.C.S.**
   (with **WHOLE LOTTA LOVE** in 1971)

5 **ARGENT**
   (with **HOLD YOUR HEAD UP** in 1972)

6 **PETER SKELLERN**
   (with **YOU'RE A LADY** in 1972)

7 **MIKE OLDFIELD**
   (with **TUBULAR BELLS (EXORCIST THEME)** in 1974)

8 **RUBETTES**
   (with **SUGAR BABY LOVE** in 1974)

9 **ROGER WHITTAKER**
   (with **THE LAST FAREWELL** in 1975)

10 **DAVID DUNDAS**
   (with **JEANS ON** in 1976)

Despite additional hits in their homeland, all these acts were consigned to the 'one-hit wonder department' in the USA, their solitary chart entry being the title listed.

TEN AMERICAN ONE-HIT WONDERS IN THE UK

1 **TOKENS**
   (with **THE LION SLEEPS TONIGHT** in 1961)

2 **RAL DONNER**
   (with **YOU DON'T KNOW WHAT YOU'VE GOT** in 1961)

3 **JIMMY REED**
   (with **SHAME SHAME SHAME** in 1964)

4 **KINGSMEN**
   (with **LOUIE LOUIE** in 1964)

5 **JOE SIMON**
   (with **STEP BY STEP** in 1973)

6 **JOHN DENVER**
   (with **ANNIE'S SONG** in 1975)

7 **IMPRESSIONS**
   (with **FIRST IMPRESSIONS** in 1975)

8 **HELEN REDDY**
   (with **ANGIE BABY** in 1975)

9 **OHIO PLAYERS**
   (with **WHO'D SHE COO** in 1976)

10 **JACKSON BROWNE**
   (with **STAY** in 1978)

All equipped with at least a handful of hits (and in some cases, a LOT of hits) in the native USA, the acts all impressed the British record buying public just once. John Denver's 'Annie's Song' was actually a UK number one, but still no hit follow-up!

TEN SONGS TO HAVE BEEN HITS IN FOUR OR MORE VERSIONS (UK)

Freddie Starr

Georgie Fame

STRANGER IN PARADISE
(Tony Bennett, Eddie Calvert, Bing Crosby, Don Cornell, Tony Martin, Four Aces)
THE STORY OF MY LIFE
(Michael Holliday, Gary Miller, Alma Cogan, Dave King)
UNCHAINED MELODY
(Al Hibbler, Jimmy Young, Righteous Brothers, Liberace, Les Baxter)
WHITE CHRISTMAS
(Bing Crosby, Mantovani, Pat Boone, Freddie Starr)
MY WAY
(Frank Sinatra, Dorothy Squires, Elvis Presley, Sex Pistols)
GARDEN OF EDEN
(Frankie Vaughan, Gary Miller, Dick James, Joe Valino)
WALK HAND IN HAND
(Tony Martin, Ronnie Carroll, Gerry & The Pacemakers, Jimmy Parkinson)
VOLARE
(Domenico Modugno, Dean Martin, Bobby Rydell, Charlie Drake, Marino Marini
SUCU SUCU
(Laurie Johnson, Nina And Frederick, Ted Heath, Joe Loss, Ping Ping & Al Verlaine)
SUNNY
(Bobby Hebb, Georgie Fame, Cher, Boney M)

Cliff Richard

143

THE MOST-RECORDED SONGS OF ALL TIME

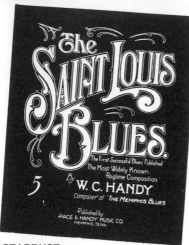

STARDUST
(Hoagy Carmichael)
ST. LOUIS BLUES
(W.C. Handy)

Definitely the most recorded pair of songs ever, both of these have been around for over half a century, and are both estimated to have clocked up more than 1,000 recorded versions.

Others with several hundred versions:–

YESTERDAY
(Paul McCartney & John Lennon)
WHITE CHRISTMAS
(Irving Berlin)
RUDOLPH THE RED-NOSED REINDEER
(Johnny Marks)
JINGLE BELLS
(J.S. Pierpont)
RELEASE ME
(Eddie Miller & Dub Williams)
MISTY
(Johnny Burke & Errol Garner)
MACK THE KNIFE (MORITAT)
(Kurt Weill/Berthold Brecht/Marc Blitzstein)
ROCK AROUND THE CLOCK
(Max C Freedman & Jimmy DeKnight)

These are just ten particularly good examples, of course; there have been many, many other songs which have been recorded hundreds of times, and proved to have such a timeless appeal that new versions continue to be made, regardless of the age of the original recording. Christmas songs, once established as standards, are particularly lucky in this respect, in that their subject matter is always topical – once a year, at least!

THE MOST PROLIFIC SONGWRITERS

Almost any active songwriter will claim to have written 'hundreds' of songs in his or her career, so nobody can accurately point to this or that tunesmith and name the most prolific of all. When it comes to the most prolific writers of SUCCESSFUL songs, however, things fall more easily into place. The ten writers or writing teams listed below have each had scores of chartmaking (or even million-selling) songs recorded either by themselves or other artists:

PAUL McCARTNEY and JOHN LENNON
JERRY LEIBER and MIKE STOLLER
EDDIE HOLLAND, LAMONT DOZIER and BRIAN HOLLAND
BURT BACHARACH
MICK JAGGER and KEITH RICHARDS
HANK WILLIAMS
CHUCK BERRY
BOB DYLAN
CAROLE KING
DOC POMUS and MORT SHUMAN

Little needs to be said about most of them, except that it now appears that a lot of ostensibly Lennon/McCartney songs were either strictly Lennon OR McCartney, with some finishing and polishing assistance from the other partner. Holland/Dozier/Holland were Motown's greatest songwriting team, responsible for a string of 1960s million-sellers by the Supremes and the

Four Tops, before departing at the end of the decade to form their own Invictus label. Doc Pomus and Mort Shuman are probably the least familiar names here, but wrote scores of 1950s/60s hits together, notably 'Surrender', 'His Latest Flame', 'Little Sister' and 'A Mess Of Blues' for Elvis Presley, 'Teenager In Love' for Dion & The Belmons, and 'Save The Last Dance For Me' for the Drifters.

TEN EXCEPTIONALLY LONG SINGLES

The advent of the 12-inch single in recent years has rather devalued this category, since the larger disc format has the capacity for more music time in the groove without loss of sound quality. There are all manner of very long disco 12-inchers of little consequence. However, the longest track known to the authors on a humble 7-inch single is:

MARRIAGEMUSIC
ROBERT FRIPP
(EG Records) – 11 minutes, 45 seconds

The longest major hit singles have been:

O SUPERMAN
Lauri Anderson
(over 8 minutes)

HEY JUDE
Beatles
(over 7 minutes)

MacARTHUR PARK
Richard Harris
(over 7 minutes)

RAPPER'S DELIGHT
Sugarhill Gang
(over 7 minutes on 7" – 15 minutes on 12")

LIKE A ROLLING STONE
Bob Dylan
(over 6 minutes)

Less well known but extremely long are:

AND YOU AND I
Yes
(over 11 minutes)

MARQUEE MOON
Television
(over 10 minutes)

MERY HOPPKINS NEVER HAD DAYS LIKE THESE
P.J. Proby
(an 8-minute B-side)

MAXIMUM PENETRATION
Maximum Penetration
(both sides of the 12" totalled 29 minutes!)

The last on the list, a 1980 jazz-funk instrumental, is listed because it is probably the longest 12-inch single ever. The tune is in two parts, the first running to around 15 minutes, and part 2 to 14 minutes. A total playing time for the disc of over 29 minutes makes it quite a bit longer than many albums! Bob Dylan's 'Like A Rolling Stone', from 1966 and the earliest example here, might almost be regarded as the first of a genre. It caused quite a stir when released, particularly on American radio, which was geared to the 2 or 3-minute single, but became such a smash hit anyway that it HAD to be played.

THE OSCAR-WINNING SONGS OF THE 1950s

THE OSCAR-WINNING SONGS OF THE 1960s

1950
MONA LISA from **CAPTAIN CAREY USA**

1951
IN THE COOL, COOL OF THE EVENING
from **HERE COMES THE GROOM**

1952
HIGH NOON from **HIGH NOON**

1953
SECRET LOVE from **CALAMITY JANE**

1954
THREE COINS IN THE FOUNTAIN
from **THREE COINS IN THE FOUNTAIN**

1955
LOVE IS A MANY-SPLENDOURED THING
from **LOVE IS A MANY-SPLENDOURED THING**

1956
WHATEVER WILL BE, WILL BE
from **THE MAN WHO KNEW TOO MUCH**

1957
ALL THE WAY
from **THE JOKER IS WILD**

1958
GIGI
from **GIGI**

1959
HIGH HOPES
from **A HOLE IN THE HEAD**

1960
NEVER ON SUNDAY
from **NEVER ON SUNDAY**

1961
MOON RIVER
from **BREAKFAST AT TIFFANY'S**

1962
DAYS OF WINE AND ROSES
from **DAYS OF WINE AND ROSES**

1963
CALL ME IRRESPONSIBLE
from **PAPA'S DELICATE CONDITION**

1964
CHIM CHIM CHEREE
from **MARY POPPINS**

1965
THE SHADOW OF YOUR SMILE
from **THE SANDPIPER**

1966
BORN FREE
from **BORN FREE**

1967
TALK TO THE ANIMALS
from **DR DOLITTLE**

1968
THE WINDMILLS OF YOUR MIND
from **THE THOMAS CROWN AFFAIR**

1969
RAINDROPS KEEP FALLING ON MY HEAD
from **BUTCH CASSIDY AND THE SUNDANCE KID**

It is a rare Academy Award winner which does not turn itself into a big pop single success as well, and all of these songs were chartbusters. Three of them belonged to Frank Sinatra ('Three Coins In The Fountain', 'All The Way' and 'High Hopes') while the artists who collected on the others were Nat 'King' Cole ('Mona Lisa'), Bing Crosby ('In The Cool, Cool, Cool Of The Evening), Frankie Laine ('High Noon'), Doris Day ('Secret Love' and 'Whatever Will Be, Will Be'), the Four Aces ('Love Is A Many-Splendoured Thing') and Billy Eckstine ('Gigi').

By the 1960s, the mainstream of pop music (thanks to rock'n'roll) had grown further away from film and show tunes than previously, and most of the songs here tended to fall into the class of material covered by the whole MOR field of ballad singers as album tracks. Nevertheless, 'Never On Sunday' had umpteen hit versions on both sides of the Atlantic; while 'Moon River' was a chart-rider for Jerry Butler (USA), Danny Williams (UK) and composer Henry Mancini (both countries); and 'The Windmills Of Your Mind' and 'Raindrops

ISAAC HAYES

THE OSCAR-WINNING SONGS OF THE 1970s

1970
FOR ALL WE KNOW
from **LOVERS AND OTHER STRANGERS**

1971
THEME FROM SHAFT
from **SHAFT**

1972
THE MORNING AFTER
from **THE POSEIDON ADVENTURE**

1973
THE WAY WE WERE
from **THE WAY WE WERE**

1974
WE MAY NEVER LOVE LIKE THIS AGAIN
from **THE TOWERING INFERNO**

1975
I'M EASY
from **NASHVILLE**

1976
EVERGREEN
from **A STAR IS BORN**

1977
YOU LIGHT UP MY LIFE
from **YOU LIGHT UP MY LIFE**

1978
LAST DANCE
from **THANK GOD IT'S FRIDAY**

1979
IT GOES LIKE IT GOES
from **NORMA RAE**

The film song Oscars are invariably won by ballads, which make Isaac Hayes' success with the staccato 'Theme From Shaft' all the more outstanding. It proved to be incredibly influential on both film and TV themes in the private eye/police/spy mode for years afterwards, with all manner of imitations and developments of its juddering guitars and stabbing brass. Most of the other tunes here became hit singles in the USA, though fewer of them in Britain; the notable international hits were 'The Way We Were' and 'Evergreen' (both by Barbra Streisand), 'For All We Know' (the Carpenters), and 'You Light Up My Life' (Debby Boone).

Keep Falling On My Head' were top 10 hits for Noel Harrison and B.J. Thomas respectively – with Sacha Distel creaming off UK success on the latter title.

TEN HIT RECORDS BY BRITISH COMEDIANS

ERNIE (THE FASTEST MILKMAN IN THE WEST)
Benny Hill
(1971)

A HARD DAY'S NIGHT
Peter Sellers
(1965)

THE BALLAD OF SPOTTY MULDOON
Peter Cook
(1965)

YING TONG SONG
Goons
(1956)

THE FUNKY GIBBON
Goodies
(1975)

RIGHT SAID FRED
Bernard Cribbins
(1962)

MAD PASSIONATE LOVE
Bernard Bresslaw
(1958)

DON'T JUMP OFF THE ROOF, DAD
Tommy Cooper
(1961)

THE UGLY DUCKLING
Mike Reid
(1975)

MY BOOMERANG WON'T COME BACK
Charlie Drake
(1961)

British comedians have a good record for success in the pop chart over the years, though few of them individually can claim consistent hit runs. Bernard Cribbins' eternally-popular 'Right Said Fred' was the second of a quick trio of successes for him in 1962, the others being 'Hole In The Ground' and 'Gossip Calypso'. Charlie Drake, too, had other successes ('Splish Splash' and 'Mr Custer'), as well as his 1961 international hit with 'Boomerang'; while the Goodies (Graeme Garden, Bill Oddie and Tim Brooke-Taylor) had a string of mid-70s chart success following 'Funky Gibbon'.

Benny Hill's 'Ernie', which reached number one at Christmas 1971, was probably the biggest comedy success ever in Britain; Hill too had had some hits earlier during the 60s with 'Garden Of Love', 'Gather In The Mushrooms' and 'Transistor Radio'.

Other comedians, of course, preferred to sing 'straight' on their records, Ken Dodd and Harry Secombe being notable examples.

TEN HITS SOME US, SOME UK BY ACTORS OR ACTRESSES

WANDRIN' STAR
Lee Marvin
(UK, 1970)

MacARTHUR PARK
Richard Harris
(USA & UK, 1968)

LET'S GET TOGETHER
Hayley Mills
(USA & UK, 1961)

DR KILDARE THEME
Richard Chamberlain
(USA & UK, 1962)

IF
Telly Savalas
(UK, 1975)

THINK IT OVER
Cheryl Ladd
(USA, 1978)

THE WAY YOU LOOK TONIGHT
Edward Woodward
(UK, 1971)

MARRIED MAN
Richard Burton
(USA, 1965)

RINGO
Lorne Greene
(USA & UK, 1964)

THE BALLAD OF THUNDER ROAD
Robert Mitchum
(USA, 1958)

What was more, in the case of Richard Harris and Richard Chamberlain at least their success started them on a mini hitmaking career as singers. Harris came back again with 'The Yard Went On Forever', 'Didn't We' and 'My Boy', while Chamberlain had eight hits in all, including remakes of 'Love Me Tender', 'All I Have To Do Is Dream' and 'True Love'.

TEN BRITISH ROCK ARTISTS WHO HAVE ALSO PURSUED ACTING CAREERS (or vice versa)

PAUL JONES
DAVID ESSEX
TOYAH WILLCOX
MIKE BERRY
JEREMY CLYDE
DENNIS WATERMAN
ADAM FAITH
HAZEL O'CONNOR
PHIL DANIELS
MARIANNE FAITHFULL

Toyah

Marianne Faithfull

Most of the above have had prominent acting roles in feature films, while several have also been active in TV roles in the UK. Dennis Waterman is primarily an actor who has also moved seriously into music. David Essex found world stardom through his roles in 'That'll Be The Day' and 'Stardust' after minor roles, while Adam Faith, who went through several unmemorable films in his early 60s pop idol days, finally found TV acting acclaim in 'Budgie' (and also, coincidentally, played in 'Stardust')

Of the lesser-known names, Jeremy Clyde (formerly half of Chad & Jeremy, purveyors of British hits to the USA with 'A Summer Song', 'Before And After', etc.), has been sighted several times in British TV plays during the 70s; while Phil Daniels, star of 'Quadrophenia' and 'Breaking Glass' (the latter with Hazel O'Connor), has recorded for RCA with his own band, though to no great commercial success as yet. Mike 'Tribute To Buddy Holly' Berry is a very familiar face on British TV these days, through 'Worzel Gummidge', 'Are You Being Served' and a variety of advertisements.

149

HIT COMMERCIALS

New Seekers

I'D LIKE TO TEACH THE WORLD TO SING
New Seekers
COCA-COLA (USA & UK)

JEANS ON
David Dundas
BRUTUS JEANS (UK)

NO MATTER WHAT SHAPE YOU STOMACH'S IN
T-Bones
ALKA-SELTZER (USA)

DANCIN' EASY
Danny Williams
MARTINI (UK)

WE'VE ONLY JUST BEGAN
Carpenters
CROCKER BANK (USA)

STEP INTO A DREAM
White Plains
BUTLIN'S HOLIDAY CAMPS (UK)

MUSIC TO WATCH GIRLS BY
Bob Crewe Generation
PEPSI-COLA (USA)

ROLLIN' ON
Cirrus
YORKIE BAR CHOCOLATE (UK)

HELLO SUMMERTIME
Bobby Goldsboro
COCA-COLA (USA & UK)

GERTCHA
Chas And Dave
COURAGE BEER (UK)

When the Cirrus single first appeared, the disc was pressed onto a rectangular slab of chocolate-coloured vinyl which slid into a sleeve designed as a large-scale replica of the Yorkie Bar wrapper.

'No Matter What Shape' and 'Music To Watch Girls By' were both instrumental hits, but in all other cases the lyrics were subtly altered on the recorded version to omit the product name and generally insert some sort of romantic substitute. No advertisment jingle can ever have had greater worldwide appeal than 'I'd Like To Teach The World To Sing', which is a familiar now as when it first appeared ten years ago. It must have been one of the best investments Coca-Cola ever made; small wonder they continue to resurrect it for modern TV ads.

COMMERCIAL HITS

As well as the hit records which have developed out of songs used in TV ads, established hits songs are also sometimes taken and reworked (often with new lyrics but usually retaining the original hit sound) into advertising jingle Some examples below of ten used in the States, and ten in Britain.

(UK)

WHAT THE WORLD NEEDS NOW IS LOVE
Jackie De Shannon
(CADBURY'S DAIRY BOX)

MEMORIES ARE MADE OF THIS
Dean Martin
(KODAK)

LET YOUR LOVE FLOW
Bellamy Brothers
(LEVIS JEANS)

YOU MAKE ME FEEL BRAND NEW
Stylistics
(CANDIDE PERFUME)

I CAN'T LET MAGGIE GO
Honeybus
(NIMBLE BREAD)

YELLOW RIVER
Christie
(YELLOW PAGES)

WOULDN'T IT BE NICE
Beach Boys
(PERSIL AUTOMATIC)

LAUGHTER IN THE RAIN
Neil Sedaka
(EARTH BORN SHAMPOO)

IN THE SUMMERTIME
Mungo Jerry
(HP SAUCE)

JE T'AIME, MOI NON PLUS
Jane Birkin & Serge Gainsbourg
(IF PERFUME)

(USA)

GOOD VIBRATIONS
Beach Boys
(SUNKIST)

UP AND AWAY
Fifth Dimension
(TWA Airlines)

JUST ONE LOOK
Hollies
(MAZDA)

(THEY LONG TO BE) CLOSE TO YOU
Carpenters
(HALLMARK GREETING CARDS)

CALIFORNIA GIRLS
Beach Boys
(CLAIROL)

SWINGTOWN
Steve Miller Band
(FORD MOTORS)

OH PRETTY WOMAN
Roy Orbison
(TONE SOAP)

FEELINGS
Morris Albert
(PACIFIC PHONE CO.)

THAT'S LIFE
Frank Sinatra
(SANYO ELECTRONICS)

THE CANDY MAN
Sammy Davis Jr.
(M&M CONFECTIONERY)

FILM HITS

YELLOW SUBMARINE
Beatles

CONVOY
C.W. McCall

ODE TO BILLIE JOE
Bobbie Gentry

ALICE'S RESTAURANT
Arlo Guthrie

**MRS BROWN YOU'VE GOT
A LOVELY DAUGHTER**
Herman's Hermits

WHITE CHRISTMAS
Bing Crosby

THAT'LL BE THE DAY
Crickets

HARPER VALLEY P.T.A.
Jeannie C Riley

**SGT. PEPPER'S LONELY
HEARTS CLUB BAND**
Beatles

COAL MINER'S DAUGHTER
Loretta Lynn

In some of the above cases, the lyrical
content of the song provided a basis for
the actual film script, as with 'Harper
Valley P.T.A.', 'Coal Miner's Daughter'
and 'Ode To Billie Joe'. Most of the other
films were built around a combination of
the song concept and the appeal of the
artist concerned – this was certainly the
case with 'Mrs. Brown', 'White Christmas
(which ironically had originally been
featured in another film, 'Holiday Inn'),
and the two Beatles spin-offs 'Yellow
Submarine' and 'Sergeant Pepper'.
'That'll Be The Day' is a rather unique
case, since the Buddy Holly & The
Crickets song basically provided a sort of
temporal inspiration for this film about
late-50s youth.

C.W. McCall

TEN HIT SONGS ORIGINALLY PREMIERED IN A TV DRAMA SHOW

TV is well-known as an excellent medium for promoting records, as witness the huge TV budgets of record companies who advertise their top-name albums on the box. A cheap and effective way of pushing a single, however, is via the rare instance in which its use within an already popular programme serves as free promotion. Such cases are few and far between, but as can be seen, the popular UK twice-weekly soap opera 'Crossroads' has an excellent track record!

'Johnny Remember Me', 'Where Are You Know' and 'Let Me Go Lover' all became number one hits, quickly after their soap-box exposure.

Stephanie De Sykes

JOHNNY REMEMBER ME
John Leyton
in **HARPER'S WEST ONE** (UK, 1961)

TEENAGE CRUSH
Tommy Sands
in **THE SINGING IDOL**
(USA 1957)

NOT TOO LITTLE, NOT TOO MUCH
Chris Sandford
in **CORONATION STREET** (UK, 1963)

ALWAYS THE LONELY ONE
Alan Drew
in **COMPACT** (UK 1963)

LET ME GO LOVER
Joan Weber
in **LET ME GO LOVER** (USA, 1954)

WHERE ARE YOU NOW
Jackie Trent
in **IT'S DARK OUTSIDE**
(UK, 1965)

START MOVIN' (IN MY DIRECTION)
Sal Mineo
in **DRUMMER MAN** (USA, 1957)

WHERE WILL YOU BE
Sue Nicholls
in **CROSSROADS** (UK, 1968)

BORN WITH A SMILE ON MY FACE
Stephanie De-Sykes
in **CROSSROADS** (UK, 1974)

TOO MUCH IN LOVE
Kate Robbins
in **CROSSROADS** (UK, 1981)

TEN COMPOSERS AND LYRICISTS OF JAMES BOND THEME MUSIC

MONTY NORMAN
JOHN BARRY
LIONEL BART
ANTHONY NEWLEY
LESLIE BRICUSSE
BURT BACHARACH
PAUL McCARTNEY
MARVIN HAMLISCH
DON BLACK
BILL CONTI

John Barry wrote the music for many of the Bond films, but the actual 'James Bond Theme' which appears in most of them was composed by Monty Norman, who handled the first of the series, 'Dr No'. Burt Bacharach scored 'Casino Royale', a film which was made completely away from the series proper, its screen rights having been sold long before. Various lyricists were responsible for individual title songs, i.e. Anthony Newley and Leslie Bricusse for 'Goldfinger', Paul McCartney for 'Live And Let Die', Lionel Bart for 'From Russia With Love' and Don Black for 'Diamonds Are Forever' and 'Thunderball'.

THE 'WINTER DANCE PARTY' TOUR OF AMERICA'S MIDWEST (JANUARY/FEBRUARY, 1959)

BUDDY HOLLY
THE BIG BOPPER
RITCHIE VALENS
DION & THE BELMONTS
FRANKIE SARDO
BOBBY VEE & THE SHADOWS
JIMMY CLANTON
FRANKIE AVALON
THE 'NEW' CRICKETS
(WAYLON JENNINGS & TOMMY ALLSUP)

The significance of this particular rock'n'roll package tour is that between the shows at Clear Lake, Iowa on 2nd February, and Moorhead, Minnesota on Feb. 3rd, Buddy Holly, Ritchie Valens and The Big Bopper were killed in a plane crash. Local high school band Bobby Vee & The Shadows were drafted in to fill the bill at Moorhead, and Clanton and Avalon both joined as replacements after the tragedy. Jennings and Allsup were Holly's backing band on the tour; they performed some of the later shows in his stead.

Frankie Avalon

THE ACTS ON THE BILL OF THE BEACH BOYS' SUMMER SPECTACULAR AT THE HOLLYWOOD BOWL ON 25th JUNE, 1966

BEACH BOYS
LOVIN' SPOONFUL
CHAD AND JEREMY
OUTSIDERS
PERCY SLEDGE
SIR DOUGLAS QUINTET
LEAVES
LOVE
CAPTAIN BEEFHEART
BYRDS

Almost foreshadowing the pop festivals of a couple of years later in its star-studded scope, this show was truly a showcase for the best American music being produced during 1966. The Byrds and Lovin' Spoonful need no introduction, nor probably the way-out Captain Beefheart (this was before his classic albums like 'Trout Mask Replica') or Arthur Lee's group Love, who were hot on the singles charts via 'My Little Red Book' and '7 And 7 Is' at the time. Percy Sledge was a soul singer who had a 1966 million-seller with 'When A Man Loves A Woman', a song whose memory has probably lasted better than that of the man himself, although he had a string of excellent follow-ups. The Sir Douglas Quintet, from Texas, also had a good mid-60s chart record with 'She' About A Mover' and 'The Rains Came', as did the Outsiders with 'Time Won't Let Me, 'Respectable', and 'Girl In Love!' Chad (Stuart) and Jeremy (Clyde) were a British duo who found their fame across the water and had five big American singles, while the Leaves took the honour of having the hit single version of the song which virtually every band in the land recorded at the time, 'Hey Joe'.

TEN ARTISTS ON THE BILL OF THE 14-HOUR TECHNICOLOUR DREAM (APRIL 29th-30th, 1967 – LONDON)

john's children

PINK FLOYD
SOFT MACHINE
PRETTY THINGS
CRAZY WORLD OF ARTHUR BROWN
TOMORROW
JOHN'S CHILDREN
SAVOY BROWN
GRAHAM BOND ORGANISATION
CHAMPION JACK DUPREE
FLIES

The first and biggest psychedelic 'happening' in England, run as a benefit for the underground newspaper 'International Times'. There were many other bands featured (often playing two-at-a-time at opposite ends of the huge Alexandra Palace hall), plus drama groups, poets and light shows. Most of the groups here have survived as names or at least as memories, if not in person. Tomorrow was led by Keith West, who went on to have a tremendous solo pop hit with 'Excerpt From A Teenage Opera'. The Flies, best remembered for a heavy, slowed-down single of the Monkees' 'I'm Not Your Steppin' Stone', were the outrage of the event, showering the audience with an unwelcome mix of flour and water, as well as a barrage of noise.

TWENTY ACTS ON THE BILL OF THE WOODSTOCK FESTIVAL (AUGUST 1969)

THE WHO
JOAN BAEZ
JEFFERSON AIRPLANE
CREEDENCE CLEARWATER REVIVAL
JIMI HENDRIX
CROSBY, STILLS AND NASH
SLY AND THE FAMILY STONE
THE BAND
TEN YEARS AFTER
RICHIE HAVENS
GRATEFUL DEAD
INCREDIBLE STRING BAND
JOHN SEBASTIAN
CANNED HEAT
ARLO GUTHRIE
MELANIE
PAUL BUTTERFIELD BLUES BAND
SHA NA NA
JOE COCKER
SANTANA

Woodstock quickly became a legend in its own time, partly due to the success of the movie and the albums which were wisely made in situ. It was most certainly a culmination of the optimistic hippy dream which had carried rock music along with it since the initial emergence of West Coast rock in 1966; everything came together at Woodstock, but nothing ever quite went right afterwards.

Sha Na Na

TEN ACTS ON THE BILL OF THE BATH FESTIVAL, SHEPTON MALLET, ENGLAND JUNE (1970)

LED ZEPPELIN
PINK FLOYD
MOODY BLUES
JEFFERSON AIRPLANE
CANNED HEAT
SANTANA
IT'S A BEAUTIFUL DAY
DONOVAN
STEPPENWOLF
JOHNNY WINTER

The Bath Festival, like the Hendrix and Dylan-headlined Isle Of Wight Festivals which were its early 70s successors, was a deliberate attempt to create a 'Woodstock in Britain'. They couldn't muster quite the array of talent (there were several smaller-name UK bands on the bill as well as the ten names above, plus a few more visiting Americans), but all the same the idea of these headliners playing together at the same event seems somewhat staggering a decade on. Rain spoilt the final evening, and particularly the Jefferson Airplane's and Moody Blues' acts, but the festival attracted a quarter of a million people into deepest Somerset, and did have at least something of the buzz which must have pervaded Woodstock.

TWENTY ACTS IN THE 'TOP 40 UNRECORDED GROUPS IN NEW YORK' FESTIVAL AT THE C.B.G.B. AND UMFUG CLUBS, JULY (1975)

BLONDIE
TALKING HEADS
SHIRTS
TELEVISION
MINK DEVILLE
HEARTBREAKERS
RAMONES
MOVIES
ANTENNA
CITY LIGHTS
JOHNNY'S DANCE BAND
ICE
MARBLES
TUFF DARTS
PRETTY POISON
JELLY ROLL
JOHN COLLINS
RAINBOW DAZE
UNCLE SAM
DEMONS

As the New Wave was just starting to flex its muscles in Britain, New York was already showcasing its own underground undercurrents. These bands were all unsigned, unrecorded, and generally unknown in the middle of 1975, even in their own home town. Some of them, of course, stayed that way – but a careful look at the first seven names on the list, at least, should show the large proportion of talent which rose to the top in this particular bowl of cream.

Talking Heads

TEN WELL-KNOWN NAMES WITH EVEN MORE FAMOUS RELATIVES

MIKE McGEAR
(brother of **PAUL McCARTNEY**)

MICKEY GILLEY
(cousin of **JERRY LEE LEWIS**)

ROBIN SARSTEDT
(brother of **EDEN KANE** and **PETER SARSTEDT**)

CARLENE CARTER
(stepdaughter of **JOHNNY CASH**)

STELLA PARTON
(sister of **DOLLY PARTON**)

KATE ROBBINS
(cousin of **PAUL McCARTNEY**)

SALLY OLDFIELD
(sister of **MIKE OLDFIELD**)

GWEN McRAE
(wife of **GEORGE McRAE**)

TIM HARDIN
(direct descendent of the western outlaw **JOHN WESLEY HARDIN**)

JESSI COLTER
(former wife of **DUANE EDDY**, now married to **WAYLON JENNINGS**)

Stella Parton, sister of Dolly Parton

Generally, there is not much attempt by related artists to cash in too directly with their more famous cousins, etc. by pushing the same surname; in fact, Mike McGear deliberately abandoned the McCartney surname to help avoid being tied to closely in the world's eyes to brother Paul's musical apron strings. The three Sarstedt brothers, however, are now all of one surname, early sixties hitmaker Eden Kane having become Clive Sarstedt in recent years. Carlene Carter, in addition to her Johnny Cash connection (because he married her mother June), is also a continuation of the famous Carter Family tradition.

TEN ACTS WHO KEPT IT IN THE FAMILY

Pointer Sisters

JACKSONS
ISLEY BROTHERS
OSMONDS
STAPLE SINGERS
CARTER FAMILY
EVERLY BROTHERS
SYLVERS
POINTER SISTERS
COWSILLS
SISTER SLEDGE

These groups were (or still are, in most cases), entirely made up of closely related members, largely brothers and/or sisters. The Cowsills, Carter Family and the Staple Singers also included one or more parent along with the younger generation. In some cases (notably the Isleys and Osmonds), younger members of the family have been brought into the group as they became old enough, replacing older brothers or sisters who left to go solo or to pursue different careers.

CHILDREN OF CLERGYMEN

ALICE COOPER
ARETHA FRANKLIN
RITA COOLIDGE
LOU RAWLS
BONNIE POINTER
GLEN CAMPBELL
MARVIN GAYE
JESSI COLTER
PAUL DAVIS
SAM COOKE

A lot of black performers are acknowledged to have come from gospel roots musically, so it is not too much of a surprise to find that Marvin Gaye, Aretha Franklin, Lou Rawls, Bonnie Pointer (and the rest of the Pointer Sisters, for that matter), and Sam Cooke were all the sons or daughters of church ministers. The white artists are less obviously of clerical upbringing, although most of those listed here do have a country music leaning, which always in itself has a religious bias. The name which stands out like a sore thumb is that of Alice Cooper, who must surely have been the archetypal prodigal son. What on earth did Dad make of all the blood, chickens and babies, one wonders?

Aretha Franklin

'BROTHERS' WHO ARE NOT REALLY BROTHERS

Righteous Brothers

RIGHTEOUS BROTHERS
(Bill Medley & Bobby Hatfield)
WALKER BROTHERS
(Scott Engel, John Maus and Gary Leeds)
BROTHERS FOUR
(Bob Glick, Mike Kirkland, Richard Foley and John Paine)
DOOBIE BROTHERS
(Pat Simmons, Tom Johnston, Jeff 'Skunk' Baxter, Tiran Porter, John Hartmann, Keith Knudsen, Michael McDonald)
ALLISONS
(known as John and Bob Allison, but actually Colin Day and Brian Alford)

Groups of brothers have long been a familiar feature of the rock landscape, adn the public usually takes them at face value. Certainly most of the best-known 'brothers' are genuine siblings – the Everlys, Isleys, Johnsons, etc. – but several well-known combinations are not related at all, as per those in the listings above, who have been picked out because they have been the most successful non-brother brothers, with at least one million selling singles apiece. Other lesser-known fraternal bands like the Soul Brothers, Ram Holder Brothers and the Soul Brothers Six almost certainly weren't the real McCoy either.

THE BEATLES' BIGGEST-SELLING SINGLES IN THE UK

THE BEATLES
PARLOPHONE RECORDS

1 **SHE LOVES YOU**
(1963)

2 **I WANT TO HOLD YOUR HAND**
(1963)

3 **CAN'T BUY ME LOVE**
(1964)

4 **I FEEL FINE**
(1964)

5 **WE CAN WORK IT OUT/DAY TRIPPER**
(1965)

6 **HELP**
(1965)

7 **HEY JUDE**
(1968)

8 **A HARD DAY'S NIGHT**
(1964)

9 **FROM ME TO YOU**
(1963)

10 **HELLO GOODBYE**
(1967)

11 **TWIST AND SHOUT EP**
(1963)

12 **MAGICAL MYSTERY TOUR EP**
(1967)

13 **TICKET TO RIDE**
(1965)

14 **GET BACK**
(1969)

15 **ALL YOU NEED IS LOVE**
(1967)

16 **PAPERBACK WRITER**
(1966)

17 **PENNY LANE/STRAWBERRY FIELDS FOREVER**
(1967)

18 **YELLOW SUBMARINE/ELEANOR RIGBY**
(1966)

19 **LET IT BE**
(1970)

20 **LADY MADONNA**
(1968)

Although virtually every single the Beatles released made the top of the charts in Britain, they didn't sell in anything like the same quantities. The top five, released at the height of Beatlemania, all sold seven-figure totals within the UK, with 'Help' also nudging that figure. The five records at the bottom of this list, by contrast, sold more modestly(!) in the region of half-a-million copies each. Note the two huge-selling extended players at numbers 11 and 12; they are easily the two biggest-selling EPs in British record history.

BIGGEST-SELLING SINGLES IN THE UK BY EX-BEATLES

1. **MULL OF KINTYRE**
   Paul McCartney & Wings
   (1977)
2. **IMAGINE**
   John Lennon
   (1975)
3. **MY SWEET LORD**
   George Harrison
   (1971)
4. **(JUST LIKE) STARTING OVER**
   John Lennon
   (1980)
5. **HAPPY CHRISTMAS (WAR IS OVER)**
   John, Yoko & Plastic Ono Band
   (1972)
6. **SILLY LOVE SONGS**
   Paul McCartney & Wings
   (1976)
7. **GIVE PEACE A CHANCE**
   John, Yoko & Plastic Ono Band
   (1969)
8. **GOODNIGHT TONIGHT**
   Paul McCartney & Wings
   (1979)
9. **LET 'EM IN**
   Paul McCartney & Wings
   (1976)
10. **WITH A LITTLE LUCK**
    Paul McCartney & Wings
    (1978)

'Mull Of Kintyre', as well documented elsewhere in this book, is the biggest-selling single of all time within the UK. John Lennon's 'Imagine' also became a million-seller when it went to number one following his tragic death; this was a period which brought huge sales for all Lennon's material (and much of the Beatles'), and also pushed his then current single '(Just Like) Starting Over' well past the half-million mark.

George Harrison has never really sold much in the way of singles in Britain as a solo artist, with the notable exception of 'My Sweet Lord', which is also nudging

seven figures in UK sales. Ringo is notable by his absence, but his 'Back Off Boogaloo' was only just squeezed out of this top ten list by 'With A Little Luck', and his 'It Don't Come Easy' is also close behind on sales.

THE TRACKS ON THE BEATLES' NEVER-RELEASED 'GET BACK, DON'T LET ME DOWN AND 12 OTHER SONGS' ALBUM (1969)

LET IT BE
SAVE THE LAST DANCE FOR ME
DON'T LET ME DOWN
MAGGIE MAE
ONE AFTER 909
TWO OF US ON OUR WAY HOME
I DIG A PONY
DIG IT
I'VE GOT A FEELING
THE LONG AND WINDING ROAD
FOR YOU BLUE
TEDDY BOY
THE WALK
GET BACK

After much delay, changing of minds, shooting of film, and remixing of the tracks by Phil Spector, much of this eventually appeared in changed form as the album 'Let It Be'. The missing cuts are to be found on bootlegs!

TEN NEVER-RELEASED BEATLES RECORDINGS

WHAT'S THE NEW MARY JANE
NOT GUILTY
PEACE OF MIND
HOW DO YOU DO IT?
LOVE OF THE LOVED
SOLDIER OF LOVE
CARABELLA
JUBILEE
TEDDY BOY
WHEN I COME TO TOWN

These songs originate from various periods in the Beatles' career. Some of them have surfaced in versions of varying quality on an assortment of bootleg albums, but none were ever released officially – nor are likely to be (although 'What's The New Mary Jane' almost made it as the B-side of an unreleased Plastic Ono Band single). 'Mary Jane' and George Harrison's song 'Not Guilty' were intended for the double white album, and included in press reports of tracks likely to appear thereon until quite shortly before the actual release. Harrison has subsequently recorded another song title 'Not Guilty' himself, although it is probably not the same number.

'How Do You Do It?' was the song George Martin bullied them into recording for their second single, but which he relented over after they had (a) played it very badly, and (b) come up with 'Please Please Me' instead. 'Love Of The Loved' was made as a publisher's demo shortly afterwards; it was probably from this that Cilla Black got the song later in 1963.

'Peace Of Mind', 'Jubilee', 'Teddy Boy' and 'When I Come To Town' are all late-60s recordings; 'Teddy Bear' should have been on the 'Get Back' album, but in fact has only ever appeared officially in a McCartney solo version in 1970. 'Carabella' and 'Soldier Of Love' are

much earlier, and actually got onto a bootleg single in the States during 1964, causing some flak for American radio stations which tried to play the songs.

TEN LENNON/McCARTNEY SONGS NEVER RECORDED (OR NEVER RELEASED) BY THE BEATLES

BAD TO ME
for **BILLY J KRAMER & THE DAKOTAS**
LIKE DREAMERS DO
for the **APPLEJACKS**
A WORLD WITHOUT LOVE
for **PETER AND GORDON**
THAT MEANS A LOT
for **P.J. PROBY**
TIP OF MY TONGUE
for **TOMMY QUICKLY**
IT'S FOR YOU
for **CILLA BLACK**
I'M IN LOVE
for the **FOURMOST**
ONE AND ONE IS TWO
for the **STRANGERS WITH MIKE SHANNON**
GOODBYE
for **MARY HOPKIN**
THINGUMMYBOB
for the **BLACK DYKE MILLS BAND**

The Beatles are known to have recorded 'Love Of The Loved' as a demo, and it is conceivable that similar demo versions of these other songs, which were covered by an assortment of artists, also existed at some time. If so, somebody has been sitting on the unheard tapes for a very long time now. The exception is probably 'Goodbye', which was a Paul McCartney solo composition specifically written for Mary Hopkin as the follow-up to 'Those Were The Days'.

TEN LABELS ON WHICH BEATLES RECORDS HAVE APPEARED IN THE USA

CAPITOL
APPLE
VEE JAY
SWAN
TOLLIE
ATCO
DECCA
MGM
UNITED ARTISTS
POLYDOR

The Beatles' early record career in the USA was extremely confused, because initially EMI's licensee in the States, Capital Records, did not take up its first option on every release, allowing the other, smaller, labels like Vee Jay and Swan to pick them up. By the time of 'I Want To Hold Your Hand' early in 1964, Capitol had its act together, and with the help of an excellent publicity campaign, pushed the record to number one. This was the cue for all the other short-term leaseholders to cash in with their Beatle products. Vee Jay had the first album and all the singles prior to 'She Loves You', and they milked these tracks virtually dry for the best part of a year, scoring huge hits with a succession of singles like 'Please Please Me' and 'Do You Want To Know A Secret', and with 'Twist And Shout' and 'Love Me Do' on the subsidiary Tollie label. Swan records had just the 'She Loves You' single, but did pretty well out of it, with a number one hit.

MGM, Atco, Decca and Polydor have at various times all had the use of tracks from the early Beatles sessions recorded in Hamburg for German Polydor. MGM had a chart hit with 'My Bonnie', and Atco a bigger one with 'Ain't She Sweet'. Finally, Apple was of course the Beatles'

own label, marketed by Capitol, while United Artists (because its parent company made the film) had the American release rights to the sountrack album from 'A Hard Day's Night'.

SONGWRITERS COVERED BY THE BEATLES

LARRY WILLIAMS
Dizzy Miss Lizzy, Slow Down, Bad Boy
CARL PERKINS
Matchbox, Everybody's Trying To Be My Baby, Honey Don't
CHUCK BERRY
Roll Over Beethoven, Little Queenie, Sweet Little Sixteen, Rock And Roll Music
GERRY GOFFIN & CAROLE KING
Chains
RAY CHARLES
Hallelujah I Love Her So, Talkin' About You
BUDDY HOLLY
Words Of Love
LITTLE RICHARD
Long Tall Sally
PHIL MEDLEY & BERT RUSSELL
Twist And Shout
MEREDITH WILSON
Til There Was You
SMOKEY ROBINSON
You Really Got A Hold On Me

As the world knows, the Beatles' songwriting abilities quickly pushed aside their needs to rely on other peoples' material; eventually, when they needed soft ballads or rousing encore rockers they could use their own ('And I Love Her;' 'I'm Down') instead of standards ('Til There Was You'; 'Long Tall Sally') The above are ten of the familiar pop writers whose songs the group did issue on record – although several of these songs, like both the Ray Charles items and two of the Jerry Lee Lewises, can only be found on the belatedly released

'Star Club' sessions from 1962. Altogether, Larry Williams or Carl Perkins probably made most in royalties from the Beatles, although because 'Twist And Shout' was a number one American single and a Number 2 British EP, Bert Russell and Phil Medley could also be in contention. Among other songwriters who had one song covered on an early Beatles album are Hal David & Burt Bacharah; Arthur Alexander; Roy Lee Johnson; Chan Romero; Meredith Wilson and Tommy Roe. To be democratic, it should be noted that 'Long Tall Sally' was actually co-written by Bumps Blackwell and Enotris Johnson as well as Little Richard Penniman.

Gene Vincent with Joe Brown

TEN ACTS APPEARING ON LOU REIZNER'S 'ALL THIS AND WORLD WAR II' ALBUM SET

ELTON JOHN
LEO SAYER
BEE GEES
ROD STEWART
FRANKIE LAINE
STATUS QUO
BROTHERS JOHNSON
HELEN REDDY
DAVID ESSEX
FOUR SEASONS

Each act on the set performs a different Beatles song. Rod Stewart and the Four Seasons had UK chart hits with their versions of 'Get Back' and 'We Can Work It Out' respectively. The album probably remains the greatest all-star assemblage of artists recording Lennon/McCartney songs ever, not being matched even by the later 'Sergeant Pepper's Lonely Hearts Club Band' soundtrack album.

BILL TOPPERS WHO HAD THE BEATLES AS A SUPPORT ACT

BRUCE CHANNEL
LITTLE RICHARD
HELEN SHAPIRO
CHRIS MONTEZ
TOMMY ROE
FRANK IFIELD
SHANE FENTON & THE FENTONES
JOE BROWN
ROYAL SHOWBAND
GENE VINCENT

These shows all took place between the Beatles' early Hamburg years and their own first tour as bill-toppers in summer 1963. Helen Shapiro and Chris Montez/Tommy Roe (jointly) headed nationwide package tours including the group in winter / spring 1962/63. Most of the other artists on this list topped a Liverpool bill on which the Beatles were the local support band; in most cases it was one show only.

163

ELVIS PRESLEY'S BIGGEST-SELLING SINGLES IN THE UK

1 IT'S NOW OR NEVER
   (1960)
2 JAILHOUSE ROCK
   (1958)
3 ARE YOU LONESOME TONIGHT?
   (1961)
4 WOODEN HEART
   (1961)
5 RETURN TO SENDER
   (1962)
6 CAN'T HELP FALLING IN LOVE/
   ROCK-A-HULA BABY
   (1962)
7 THE WONDER OF YOU
   (1970)
8 SURRENDER
   (1961)
9 WAY DOWN
   (1977)
10 ALL SHOOK UP
   (1957)

This listing represents exactly half of Elvis' chart-topping British hits. 'It's Now Or Never', top for nine weeks at the end of 1960, was easily his biggest UK success, and his only million-seller on UK sales alone. As with the Beatles, all his available singles continue to sell steadily to new generations of fans, and all the sales totals represented here are actually still climbing.

TEN UNISSUED ELVIS PRESLEY RECORDINGS

TENNESSEE SATURDAY NIGHT
SATISFIED
HUSKY DUSKY DAY
DAINTY LITTLE MOONBEAM
PLANTATION ROCK
THE LADY LOVES ME
(duet with Ann-Margret)
DOMINIC
SIGNS OF THE ZODIAC
(duet with Marilyn Mason)
COME OUT, COME OUT
POOR MAN'S GOLD

For an artist with a 23-year recording career, Elvis surprisingly proved to have a comparatively small legacy of unreleased material remaining after his death. Most of this has subsequently appeared on record, and although a lot of unissued takes and remakes of already-released songs still remain in the can, the list above represents the bulk of what remains unheard in the way of 'new' songs.

The first two tracks were recorded for Sun in 1955, and their non-release after all this time suggests that the masters have either been irretrievably lost or are of very poor quality. 'Poor Man's Gold' is an early 70s studio track, while the other titles all represent leftover songs from film soundtracks, and are largely light on both quality and real interest value. The exception is probably the comedy duet with Anne-Margret from 'Viva Las Vegas', 'The Lady Loves Me', for which Presley fans have waited since 1964 to hear on record, and may yet be rewarded.

TEN ARTISTS WITH HITS FROM COVER VERSIONS OF ELVIS PRESLEY SONGS

TERRY STAFFORD
Suspicion

RAL DONNER
The Girl of My Best Friend

JOE DOWELL
Wooden Heart

JOHN SCHNEIDER
It's Now Or Never

RY COODER
Little Sister

BILL BLACK'S COMBO
Don't Be Cruel

ANDY WILLIAMS
Can't Help Falling In Love

RICHARD CHAMBERLAIN
Love Me Tender

GILLAN
Trouble

WANDA JACKSON
Let's Have A Party

As with the Beatles, there was no way that Presley in his heyday was going to be beaten by a cover version of one of his singles, but various artists have benefitted from time to time by either borrowing his album tracks, or else reviving erstwhile Elvis hits some years later. The most recent artists to do the latter have been John Schneider (of 'Dukes Of Hazard' fame) in the USA, and Gillan in Britain, but the ploy also worked for Ry Cooder in 1979, Richard Chamberlain in 1962, Wanda Jackson in 1960, and Presley's own former bass player Bill Black in the same year.

Joe Dowell had an American chart-topper in 1961 with 'Wooden Heart', thanks to the fact that Elvis' European chart-topping version of the same stayed on the 'G.I. Blues' soundtrack LP in the States. Ral Donner's cover version of an 'Elvis Is Back' album track 'Girl Of My Best Friend' was followed by several further hits by Donner (notably 'You Don't Know What You've Got') on which he developed an uncannily Presley-like style, which fooled several people at the time into thinking Elvis was making some extra bucks by putting out a second string of hits under a pseudonym!

TEN ARTISTS WHO HAVE DUETTED VOCALLY WITH ELVIS PRESLEY

JERRY LEE LEWIS
Just A Little Talk With Jesus
(1956)

CARL PERKINS
Peace In The Valley
(1956)

HOPE LANGE
Husky Dusky Day
(1960)

ANN-MARGRET
The Lady Loves Me
(1963)

DONNA DOUGLAS
Petunia The Gardener's Daughter
(1965)

WILL HUTCHINS
Who Needs Money?
(1967)

NANCY SINATRA
There Ain't Nothing Like A Song
(1967)

MARILYN MASON
Signs Of The Zodiac
(1968)

RONNIE MILSAP
Don't Cry Daddy
(1969)

SHERRILL NEILSEN
Softly As I Leave You
(1977)

The tracks with Jerry Lee Lewis and Carl Perkins are amongst several such duets from the legendary 'Million Dollar Quartet' jam sessions at Sun Records in

Memphis, in December 1956. Half an hour's worth of the session has finally been issued on an album recently. The next six duets are all from movies ('Wild In The Country', 'Viva Las Vegas', 'Frankie And Johnny', 'Clambake', 'Speedway' and 'The Trouble With Girls', in that order), and most of them have never been considered worthy of official release on record. The 'Don't Cry Daddy' duet with blind country star Ronnie Milsap is by far the best (and best-selling) example of Presley sharing a microphone with somebody else. Finally, the Sherrill Neilson cut is a real oddity; recorded at one of his last stage shows, it features the girl singing the old Matt Monro hit while Presley weaves a spoken monologue around it.

Chet Atkins

TEN ELVIS PRESLEY BACKING MUSICIANS

SCOTTY MOORE (guitar)
HANK GARLAND (guitar)
CHET ATKINS (guitar)
JAMES BURTON (guitar)
BILL BLACK (bass)
BOB MOORE (bass)
D.J. FONTANA (drums)
HAL BLAINE (drums)
FLOYD CRAMER (piano)
GLEN D HARDIN (piano)

Scotty Moore, Bill Black and D.J. Fontana are probably the best-known line-up of Presley backing musicians; it was they who accompanied his early Sun recordings and also backed him on the tumultuous American TV appearances which helped to skyrocket his career in 1956. James Burton, a guitar star in his own right and once the stalwart of Rick Nelson's band, handled lead guitar chores through Elvis' 'live performance' period from the tail-end of the 60s until his death in 1977. Ex-Cricket Glen Hardin was around at the same time on keyboards, and following Presley's death both he and Burton moved on to form the nucleus of Emmylou Harris' Hot Band.

TEN MEMBERS OF THE VENTURES

DON WILSON (guitar)
BOB BOGLE (guitar)
NOKIE EDWARDS (lead guitar)
JERRY McGEE (lead guitar)
HOWIE JOHNSON (drums)
MEL TAYLOR (drums)
JOHNNY DURRILL (keyboards)
HARVEY MANDEL (guitar)
JOE BARILE (percussion)
JACKIE KELSO (saxophone)

America's most enduring instrumental rock group (first hit in 1960, and still going now some hundred-odd albums later), the Ventures have always revolved around guitarists Bob Bogle and Don Wilson, whilst Nokie Edwards and Mel Taylor have also been part of the group for most of its life. Guitarist Harvey Mandel and sax player Jackie Kelso have never been official band members, but both have played extensively on Ventures studio recordings.

Bruce Welch

Hank Marvi

The Ventures

TEN MEMBERS OF THE SHADOWS

HANK B MARVIN (lead guitar)
BRUCE WELCH (rhythm guitar)
JET HARRIS (bass)
TONY MEEHAN (drums)
BRIAN BENNETT (drums)
BRIAN LOCKING (bass)
JOHN ROSTILL (bass)
JOHN FARRAR (rhythm guitar/bass)
ALAN HAWKSHAW (keyboards)
ALAN JONES (bass)

Marvin, Welch and Bennett have long been (and remain) the pivot of the Shadows, though it was actually the first four names on the list who scored in 1960 with 'Apache' and recorded the group's next five hits. The longest-resident bass player was John Rostill, who died in a studio accident some years after leaving the Shadows in the late 60s. Since his departure, the group has had no official resident bass player, although Alan Jones has virtually made the post his own on live work in recent years.

John Farrar

TEN MEMBERS OF THE CRICKETS

BUDDY HOLLY
JERRY ('IVAN') ALLISON
JOE B MAULDIN
SONNY CURTIS
NIKI SULLIVAN
EARL SINKS
JERRY NAYLOR
GLEN D HARDIN
DAVID BOX
RIC GRECH

The Crickets' name spanned some twenty years on record, though they underwent many almost total personnel changes through that period, the only constant fixture being drummer Jerry Allison. The original star of the group was its first leader and vocalist Buddy Holly. Jerry Naylor and Sonny Curtis, both later to become major country music artists, were the group's vocal mainstay on its post-Holly hits. Bass player for the final albums in the 70s was Englishman Ric Grech.

Buddy Holly

TEN MUSICIANS WHO HAVE PLAYED IN JOHN MAYALL'S BANDS

ERIC CLAPTON
PETER GREEN
MICK FLEETWOOD
JOHN McVIE
AYNSLEY DUNBAR
MICK TAYLOR
DICK HECKSTALL-SMITH
KEEF HARTLEY
JACK BRUCE
HUGHIE FLINT

John Mayall's blues band line-ups of the sixties were the breeding ground for most of the (originally) blues-oriented rock musicians to emerge from Britain in the second half of that decade. The guitarwork of Clapton and Green respectively highlighted Mayall's two most commercially successful albums, 'Bluesbreakers' and 'A Hard Road'.

Mary Wilson

TEN MEMBERS OF THE SUPREMES

DIANA ROSS
MARY WILSON
FLORENCE BALLARD
CINDY BIRDSONG
SCHERRIE PAYNE
JEAN TERRELL
SUSAYE GREENE
BARBARA MARTIN
LYNDA LAWRENCE
KAREN JACKSON

The classic Supremes line-up which produced the hits of the 'Where Did Our Love Go'/'Baby Love'/'You Keep Me Hangin' On' years consisted of the three girls at the top of the list. When Diana Ross departed in 1970, Jean Terrell (sister of boxer Ernie) became lead singer, and took the group through a second string of hits like 'Stoned Love' and 'Nathan Jones'. Personnel changes were more frequent through the late 70s, with only founder member Mary Wilson hanging on in to provide continuity with the great early days.

Peter Green

TEN MEMBERS OF THE FOUR SEASONS

FRANKIE VALLI
BOB GAUDIO
NICK MASSI
TOMMY DeVITO
JOE LONG
DIMITRI CALLAS
GERRY POLCI
DON CICCONE
LEE SHAPIRO
JOHN PAIVA

The first four names formed the original hitmaking Four Seasons line-up from 1962-65, but since the later sixties the personnel changes have been fairly regular, with only Frankie Valli (and usually Bob Gaudio in a songwriting or production capacity at least) providing continuity. The group stabilised as the last four names on the list (plus Valli) for their huge hits 'Who Loves You?' and 'December '63' in the mid and late 70s.

Johnny Moore

TEN MEMBERS OF THE DRIFTERS

CLYDE McPHATTER
BILL PINCKNEY
BOBBY HENDRICKS
GERHART THRASHER
JOHNNY MOORE
BEN E KING
RUDY LEWIS
CHARLES THOMAS
BUTCH LEAKE
BILL FREDERICKS

The most enduring black music group name of all, the Drifters spanned almost three decades of recording, inevitably changing their personnel many, many times. Johnny Moore, who first sang with the group in the mid-50s and then led them in the late sixties and their 'British-based' period fo the seventies, is probably the strongest link in a long, long chain.

TEN SIDEMEN USED BY THE ROLLING STONES

RY COODER
BILLY PRESTON
JACK NITZSCHE
PHIL SPECTOR
MAC REBENNACK
JIM PRICE
HARVEY MANDEL
MEL COLLINS
JIM HORN
(and of course) **IAN STEWART**

The Stones have used additional musicians on several occasions through the years both on stage and record, either on keyboards or brass/woodwind instrument, to 'fatten' the group's basic guitar/drums sounds. This listing is not exhaustive, but covers the best-known 'guest' names.

Ry Cooder

TEN MEMBERS OF GINGER BAKER'S AIRFORCE (1970)

GINGER BAKER
DENNY LAINE
RIC GRECH
STEVIE WINWOOD
GRAHAM BOND
PHIL SEAMAN
HAROLD McNAIR
CHRIS WOOD
BUD BEADLE
STEVE GREGORY

Probably the largest and most unwieldy product of the 'supergroup' syndrome, Baker employed some 15 musicians and vocalists in all, for two albums and (very crowded) stage work.

172

TEN MEMBERS OF THE PLASTIC ONO BAND

JOHN LENNON
YOKO ONO
KLAUS VOORMAN
RINGO STARR
ALAN WHITE
JIM KELTNER
GEORGE HARRISON
NICKY HOPKINS
ERIC CLAPTON
BOBBY KEYS

John Lennon's Plastic Ono Band was always something of a pick-up band, usinig specific groups of musicians along with Lennon and Yoko Ono for particular shows or albums – hence the appearances in the list of Ringo, George Harrison, and Eric Clapton (who played on the 'Live Peace In Toronto' album), along with many recognised session players.

Eric Clapton

John Lennon and Yoko Ono

SAME TITLE, BUT TWO COMPLETELY DIFFERENT SONGS

Bob Welch

HERE COMES THE NIGHT Beach Boys/
HERE COMES THE NIGHT Ben E King

LONELY BOY Paul Anka/
LONELY BOY Andrew Gold

IT'S TOO LATE Carole King/
IT'S TOO LATE Wilson Pickett

WHAT IN THE WORLD'S COME OVER
YOU Jack Scott/
WHAT IN THE WORLD'S COME OVER
YOU Rockin' Berries

MISS YOU Rolling Stones/
MISS YOU Jimmy Young

TEDDY BEAR Elvis Prelsey/
TEDDY BEAR Red Sovine

TRAGEDY Bee Gees/
TRAGEDY Thomas Wayne

EBONY EYES Bob Welch/
EBONY EYES Everly Brothers

MY LOVE Petula Clark/
MY LOVE Paul McCartney & Wings

I LOVE YOU Cliff Richard/
I LOVE YOU Donna Summer

These are ten (or twenty) examples chosen for the familiarity of one or both of the songs in each pair, but they serve as just an example of a common phenomenon – not a greatly surprising one in view of the comparatively restricted number of topics about which songs get written, and of the way certain phrases (and words) have a neat commercial ring which lends them to frequent use. There must be a contender for the title most used for different songs, although we haven't attempted to find it. A rather unexpected one-word offering which has come up at least three different times is 'Fire'.   Arthur Brown, the Ohio Players and Bruce Springsteen have all had completely different songs bearing this most unlikely word as their title.

SUCCESSFUL NEW NAMES

SHANE FENTON – ALVIN STARDUST
PAUL RAVEN – GARY GLITTER
GERRY DORSEY – ENGELBERT HUMPERDINCK
DAVY JONES – DAVID BOWIE
DRIFTERS – SHADOWS
JOHNNY CYMBAL – DEREK
N' BETWEENS – SLADE
SPECTRES – STATUS QUO
HIGH NUMBERS – WHO
DEAN FORD & THE GAYLORDS – MARMALADE

These case histories vary. Two of the acts, Shane Fenton and Johnny Cymbal, had it hit records in these earlier incarnations ('I'm A Moody Guy' and 'Mr Bass Man' in 1961 and 1963 respectively) before disappearing for several years to come back with more hits in their new guises (Derek had a US hit with 'Cinnamon' in 1968). For the rest, it was definitely a question of 'change of name – change of luck' – although only in one case (the Who) did the very first single they released with a new name bring them a chart success. An interesting sideline to this is that obscure records by the Spectres, N' Betweens, Davy Jones, Paul Raven and the High Numbers are now sought-after collectors items in the eyes of avid fans of the acts in later superstar guises.

Elkie Brooks
of Vinegar Joe

NO SUCH PERSON IN THE BAND

DR FEELGOOD
JETHRO TULL
HENRY COW
URIAH HEEP
DR HOOK
VINEGAR JOE
MOLLY HATCHET
LYNYRD SKYNYRD
MARSHALL TUCKER BAND
DEREK & THE DOMINOES

It is not too unusual for a group or band to name itself after one individual, or to highlight one individual from their line-up – not many people remember, for instance, that Fleetwood Mac was originally Peter Green's Fleetwood Mac when first formed. Less frequent, but nonetheless throwing up some familiar names, as shown above, is the instance where a band is apparently named after an individual, but where that individual does not actually exist. This is particularly confusing for people outside the world of rock appreciation – national news reporters, etc. – who may turn up for an interview and ask to see Derek, Molly, Henry or Mr. Tucker. Much of the population of Britain would probably tell you that the fellow who plays a flute and sings standing on one leg is called Jethro Tull, rather than Ian Anderson.

TEN NICELY-MATCHED A AND B SIDES OF SINGLES

ARE YOU LONESOME TONIGHT/
I GOTTA KNOW
Elvis Presley

WHO'S MAKING LOVE/
I'M TRYING
Johnnie Taylor

WHICH WAY DO I GET HOME/
ON A GREEN LINE BUS
Splinter

MARY MARY/
THE COMPLETE MAN
Cat Stevens

TRY MY WORLD/
NO THANKS
Georgie Fame

DON'T MESS UP A GOOD THING/
JERK LOOSE
Fontella Bass & Bobby McClure

DEAR DELILAH/THE DEAD BOOT
Grapefruit

NEED YOUR LOVE SO BAD/
STOP MESSIN' AROUND
Fleetwood Mac

GO/STOP
Sounds Incorporated

I'M A MAN/CAN'T GET ENOUGH OF IT
Spencer Davis Group

A little imagination from artists or their A&R men could provide plenty more of these and no doubt there are many further hilarious couplings lurking amongst the rich legacy of past releases.

Johnnie Taylor

TEN ARTISTS WHO HAVE DIED IN PLANE CRASHES

BUDDY HOLLY
RITCHIE VALENS
THE BIG BOPPER
PATSY CLINE
COWBOY COPAS
JIM REEVES
OTIS REDDING
JIM CROCE
RONNIE VAN ZANT
(Lynyrd Skynyrd)
STEVE GAINES
(Lynyrd Skynyrd)

A grisly statistic concerned with deaths in the air is the multiplicity involved in the incidents. All ten artists listed here died in just six crashes: Holly, Valens and Bopper (real name J.P. Richardson) in 1959, Cline and Copas (along with another country star, Hawkshaw Hawkins) in 1963, Reeves in 1964, Redding in 1967 (along with all but one member of his backing group the Bar-Kays), Croce in 1973, and the members of Lynyrd Skynyrd in 1977. The rest of the band were also involved in this last crash, but survived with injuries to recover.

the case of Elvis Presley at least, being directly traceable to massive drug abuse.

Of the less familiar names in the listing, Florence Ballard was one of the three original Supremes, although she died some time after leaving the trio. Slim Harpo was an influential bluesman (the Rolling Stones, in particular, owed much to his style), while Chris Kenner and Clyde McPhatter were also major R&B performers, McPhatter being for some years the lead singer of the Drifters before following a solo career. Lowell George was the leader of Little Feat, while Dorsey Burnette was the brother of hitmaker Johnny (who had died 15 years earlier in a boating accident), and recorded in his own right as well as composing several hits for Ricky Nelson.

Marc Bolan

CARDIAC ARRESTS

SLIM HARPO (1970)
JIM MORRISON (1971)
CLYDE McPHATTER (1972)
CHRIS KENNER (1976)
FLORENCE BALLARD (1976)
ELVIS PRESLEY (1977)
VAN McCOY (1979)
LOWELL GEORGE (1979)
DORSEY BURNETTE (1979)

All these artists died of heart attacks, presumably brought about by a variety of other medical causes, and certainly in

DEATH ON THE ROAD

EDDIE COCHRAN (1960)
JOHNNY HORTON (1960)
JESSE BELVIN (1960)
RICHARD FARINA (1966)
BILLY STEWART (1970)
EARL GRANT (1970)
DUANE ALLMAN (1971)
BERRY OAKLEY (1972)
CLARENCE WHITE (1973)
MARC BOLAN (1977)

Of these, Cochran, Horton, Belvin, Stewart, Grant and Bolan all died in (or later as the result of injuries received in) car crashes. Duane Allman and Berry Oakley, both members of the Allman Brothers band, died in motorcycle smashes, as did folksinger/songwriter Richard Fariña (who by a weird coincidence, had his song 'Pack Up Your Sorrows' recorded by Joan Baez at around the same time.) Clarence White, a late-era member of the Byrds, was killed on the road after being hit by a truck.

DO UNTO YOURSELF

DONNY HATHAWAY
PETE HAM
JOHNNY ACE
JOE MEEK
PHIL OCHS
IAN CURTIS
PIGPEN (RON McKERNAN)
TERRY KATH
PAUL WILLIAMS

Performers who died at their own hand. It's perhaps gratifying that we couldn't find a tenth name for the list. Seven of these were actual suicides, but Terry Kath of Chicago and Johnny Ace both died of accidentally self-inflicted gunshot wounds – the latter whilst playing Russian Roulette. Paul Williams was one of the many lead singers of the Temptations – not the diminutive songwriter and sometime actor of the same name.

TEN DEATH SONGS

LEADER OF THE PACK
Shangri-Las
LAST KISS
J. Frank Wilson & The Cavaliers
TEEN ANGEL
Mark Dinning
TELL LAURA I LOVE HER
Ricky Valance
TERRY
Twinkle

MOODY RIVER
Pat Boone
EBONY EYES
Everly Brothers
D.O.A.
Bloodrock
A YOUNG GIRL (OF SIXTEEN)
Noel Harrison
THE NIGHT THE LIGHTS WENT OUT IN GEORGIA
Vicki Lawrence

Death, being a permanent fact of life, as it were, has been a natural ingredient in many songs and many hit records. It usually occurs in a song as part of a violent melodrama involving love, revenge or irony (or in the real classic of the genre, all three.) Those listed above are probably the best-known examples of songs which became hits largely through their use of the death element as a hook. In six of the first seven songs above, the main character in the song (the boy or girl-friend of the first-person narrator) dies tragically in the air or on the road (or in the case of 'Teen Angel', on the railroad tracks.) The exception is 'Moody River', in which the girl drowns herself in a river. 'The Night The Lights, etc.' is a tawdry eternal triangle story with everybody in sight being bumped off for revenge or unrequited love. 'A Young Girl' is a sort of female Rake's Progress, with the girl ending up dead by the side of the road. 'D.O.A.' (or 'Dead On Arrival') is in a class of its own, being the first person narration of an accident victim as he ebbs fast in the back of the ambulance whisking him vainly to hospital; it must be heard to be believed.

Shangri-Las

177

TEN ARTISTS WHO HAD MORE THAN TWENTY HITS WITHOUT EVER REACHING NO.1 (USA)

Duane Eddy

B.B. King

JOHNNY CASH
(highest position: No. 2)
IMPRESSIONS
(highest position: No.4)
JACK JONES
(highest position: No.14)
B.B. KING
(highest position: No.15)
JOHNNY TILLOTSON
(highest position: No.2)
FATS DOMINO
(highest position: No.4)
JAMES BROWN
(highest position: No.2)
BOBBY RYDELL
(highest position: No.2)
JIM REEVES
(highest position: No.2)
DUANE EDDY
(highest position: No.4)

James Brown is the all-time champ here. Having had getting on for a hundred American Top 100 entries between 1956 and the present, but without ever quite going all the way to the top. His biggest success, reaching number 2, was 'I Got You (I Feel Good)' at the end of 1965.

The highest-charted discs for the others on the list above were: 'A Boy Named Sue' (Johnny Cash); 'It's All Right' (Impressions); 'Poetry In Motion' (Johnny Tillotson); 'Wives And Lovers' (Jack Jones); 'The Thrill Is Gone' (B.B. King); 'Because They're Young' (Duane Eddy); 'Blueberry Hill' (Fats Domino); 'Wild One' (Bobby Rydell); and 'He'll Have to Go' (Jim Reeves).

TEN ARTISTS WHO HAD MORE THAN TWENTY HITS WITHOUT EVER REACHING NO.1 (UK)

Billy Fury

Gladys Knight and the Pips

BILLY FURY
(highest position: No.2)
NAT 'KING' COLE
(highest position: No.2)
THE WHO
(highest position: No.2)
FATS DOMINO
(highest position: No.3)
DUANE EDDY
(highest position: No.2
GLADYS KNIGHT & THE PIPS
(highest position: No.4)
BRENDA LEE
(highest position: No.3)
RICKY NELSON
(highest position: No.2)
GENE PITNEY
(highest position: No.2)
STEVIE WONDER
(highest position: No.2)

Nat 'King' Cole, Stevie Wonder and Billy Fury have had 29, 29 and 26 British Chart Hits respectively, without managing to hit the top slot – although Cole's 'Mona Lisa' may well have done so, had the UK Charts been in existence when it was released. Nat reached No. 2 with 'Pretend' in 1953; 'Smile' in 1954; and 'When I Fall In Love' in 1957. Stevie's runner-up-placed hits were 'Yester Me Yester You Yesterday' in 1969, 'Sir Duke' in 1977, and 'Lately' in 1981. Finally, Billy Furry made second place with 'I'd Never Find Another You' in 1962.

The highest placed hits for the others on the list above were 'Bluberry Hill' (Fats Domino); 'Speak To Me Pretty' (Brenda Lee); 'My Generation' and 'I'm A Boy' (The Who); 'Hello Mary Lou' (Ricky Nelson); 'Baby Don't Change Your Mind' (Gladys Knight); 'I'm Gonna Be Strong' and 'Nobody Needs Your Love' (Gene Pitney); and 'Because They're Young' (Duane Eddy).

THE NUMBER ONE CHRISTMAS SINGLES OF THE 1950s

Conway Twitty

Pat Bo[...]

(USA)

1950 **THE TENNESSEE WALTZ**
Patti Page

1951 **CRY**
Johnnie Ray

1952 **I SAW MOMMY KISSING SANTA CLAUS**
Jimmy Boyd

1953 **OH MY PAPA**
Eddie Fisher

1954 **MR SANDMAN**
Chordettes

1955 **SIXTEEN TONS**
Tennessee Ernie Ford

1956 **SINGING THE BLUES**
Guy Mitchell

1957 **APRIL LOVE**
Pat Boone

1958 **THE CHIPMUNK SONG (CHRISTMAS DON'T BE LATE)**
Chipmunks

1959 **WHY**
Frankie Avalon

(UK)

1952 **HERE IN MY HEART**
Al Martino

1953 **ANSWER ME**
Frankie Laine

1954 **LET'S HAVE ANOTHER PARTY**
Winifred Atwell

1955 **CHRISTMAS ALPHABET**
Dickie Valentine

1956 **JUST WALKIN' IN THE RAIN**
Johnnie Ray

1957 **MARY'S BOY CHILD**
Harry Belafonte

1958 **IT'S ONLY MAKE BELIEVE**
Conway Twitty

1959 **WHAT DO YOU WANT**
Adam Faith

Christmas week is traditionally the biggest sales week in the calendar for records (for obvious reasons), meaning that the disc which happens to be the best-seller of the moment stands a strong chance of being the biggest seller of the year. This was probaly not quite so much the case back in the 1950s, but certainly all the records listed above were exceptionally strong sellers – 'Mary's Boy Child' was one of Britain's few pre-Beatles million-selling hits. Ironically, on only two occasions in each country during the 50s was the Christmas best-seller actually a Christmas song.

(NB: There are no titles for 1950 and 1951 in the UK because the charts were not in existence then.)

THE NUMBER ONE CHRISTMAS SINGLES OF THE 1960s

Diana Ross & The Supremes

(USA)

1960 **ARE YOU LONESOME TONIGHT**
Elvis Presley

1961 **THE LION SLEEPS TONIGHT**
Tokens

1962 **TELSTAR**
Tornados

1963 **DOMINIQUE**
Singing Nun

1964 **I FEEL FINE**
Beatles

1965 **OVER AND OVER**
Dave Clark Five

1966 **I'M A BELIEVER**
Monkees

1967 **HELLO GOODBYE**
Beatles

1968 **I HEARD IT THROUGH THE GRAPEVINE**
Marvin Gaye

1969 **SOMEDAY WE'LL BE TOGETHER**
Diana Ross & The Supremes

Cliff Richard in pantomime

1967 **HELLO GOODBYE**
Beatles

1968 **LILY THE PINK**
Scaffold

1969 **TWO LITTLE BOYS**
Rolf Harris

(UK)

1960 **IT'S NOW OR NEVER**
Elvis Presley

1961 **STRANGER ON THE SHORE**
Mr Acker Bilk

1962 **THE NEXT TIME**
Cliff Richard

1964 **I FEEL FINE**
Beatles

1965 **WE CAN WORK IT OUT/ DAY TRIPPER**
Beatles

1966 **GREEN GREEN GRASS OF HOME**
Tom Jones

Not a Christmas song in sight at number one during this decade; in fact, Christmas hits generally became extremely scarce, to enjoy a notable revival on single in Britain during the 1970s.

From 1963 onwards, it became habitual for the Beatles to release a new single to close the year out, and these generally settled down as the Christmas number one hit. The Beatles' 'We Can Work It Out' didn't fail to repeat its UK success in the States in 1965 – it simply made the chart-top a week later, thanks to particularly strong sales by major UK rivals of the time the Dave Clark Five (with a single which barely scraped the charts at all in Britain!)

THE NUMBER ONE CHRISTMAS SINGLES OF THE 1970s

(USA)

1970 **MY SWEET LORD**
George Harrison

1971 **BRAND NEW KEY**
Melanie

1972 **ME AND MRS JONES**
Billy Paul

1973 **THE MOST BEAUTIFUL GIRL**
Charlie Rich

1974 **LUCY IN THE SKY
WITH DIAMONDS**
Elton John

1975 **I WRITE THE SONGS**
Barry Manilow

1976 **YOU DON'T HAVE TO
BE A STAR**
Marilyn McCoo & Billy Davis Jr.

1977 **HOW DEEP IS YOUR LOVE**
Bee Gees

1978 **LE FREAK**
Chic

1979 **ESCAPE (THE PINA
COLADA SONG)**
Rupert Holmes

Billy P

(UK)

1970 **WHEN I'M DEAD AND GONE**
McGuiness Flint

1971 **ERNIE (THE FASTEST
MILKMAN IN THE WEST)**
Benny Hill

1972 **LONG-HAIRED LOVER
FROM LIVERPOOL**
Little Jimmy Osmond

1973 **MERRY XMAS EVERYBODY**
Slade

1974 **LONELY THIS CHRISTMAS**
Mud

1975 **BOHEMIAN RHAPSODY**
Queen

1976 **WHEN A CHILD IS BORN**
Johnny Mathis

1977 **MULL OF KINTYRE**
Wings

1978 **MARY'S BOY CHILD/
OH MY LORD**
Boney M

1979 **ANOTHER BRICK IN THE WALL**
Pink Floyd

Not a lot in common between the UK and
US number ones of these Christmas
weeks, although some of these records
(ie 'My Sweet Lord' and 'Another Brick In
The Wall') did repeat their success on the
alternate side of the Atlantic on a later
date. Christmas lyrics returned in a big
way in Britain (for four chart-toppers out
of ten), while the American number ones
are notable for their apparent complete
lack of unifying factor (except big sales).

182

THE MOST CENSORED RECORDS OF ALL TIME (UK)

The most consistently censored series of big-selling hits most definitely belongs to double-entendre reggae artist Judge Dread. Each single below was a solid chart success despite being totally banned from airplay by the BBC and other stations – and from stock by some of the high street retail chains:

BIX SIX
(August 1972)

BIG SEVEN
(December 1972)

BIG EIGHT
(April 1973)

JE T'AIME (MOI NON PLUS)
(July 1975)

BIG TEN
(September 1975)

CHRISTMAS IN DREADLAND/COME OUTSIDE
(December 1975)

THE WINKLE MAN
(May 1976)

Y VIVA SUSPENDERS
(August 1976)

5th ANNIVERSARY EP
(April 1977)

UP WITH THE COCK
(January 1978)

Judge Dread

TEN BANNED RECORDS

1 **TIMOTHY BUOYS**
   Buoys
   (Cannibalism)

2 **A DAY IN THE LIFE**
   Beatles
   (Drugs)

3 **WORKING CLASS HERO**
   John Lennon
   (Naughty Word)

4 **EVE OF DESTRUCTION**
   Barry McGuire
   (Apocalyptic Statement)

5 **GOD SAVE THE QUEEN**
   Sex Pistols
   (Insult to Royalty)

6 **EIGHT MILES HIGH**
   Byrds
   (Drugs)

7 **GIVE IRELAND BACK TO THE IRISH**
   Wings
   (Politics)

8 **MURDER OF LIDDLE TOWERS**
   Angelic Upstarts
   (Anti-Police)

9 **WE LOVE THE PIRATE STATIONS**
   Roaring Sixties
   (Guess)

10 **99% IS SHIT**
   Cash Pussies
   (A Bit of Everything)

A second helping of the banned-list, with ten more discs which the BBC in particular didn't like. 'Timothy' is amazing, relating how two survivors of a mine cave-in eat their third companion to stay alive!

TEN SONGS WHICH WERE BANNED, NEARLY BANNED, OR SHOULD HAVE BEEN BANNED

Lou Reed

SATURDAY NITE AT THE DUCKPOND
Cougars
(for being a bastardisation of
Tchaikovsky's 'Swan Lake')

ASIA MINOR
Kokomo
(for being a bastardisation of
Grieg's 1st piano concerto)

A ROSE AND A BABY RUTH
George Hamilton
(for advertising a brand name chocolate
bar)

HOT ROD LINCOLN
Johnny Bond
(for advertising a brand name car)

A BOY NAMED SUE
Johnny Cash
(it had the phrase 'Son of a Bitch'
bleeped out)

LOLA
Kinks
(It had the word 'Coca' deleted and
replaced by 'Cherry')

IT'S NOW OR NEVER
Elvis Presley
(Its release was delayed for six months
because of problems over the copyright
of the melody)

NIGHT
Jackie Wilson
(It was never released in the UK because
of a problem over the copyright)

A WALK ON THE WILD SIDE
Lou Reed
(An oblique sexual reference)

WET DREAM
Max Romeo
(Because of certain sexual connotations)

Some of these (Cougars, Kokomo, Max
Romeo) were actually banned by BBC
radio for the reasons stated, while 'Lola'
was specifically amended to avoid such a
ban. 'A Rose And A Baby Ruth' and 'Hot
Rod Lincoln' were re-recorded as 'A
Rose And A *Candy Bar*' and 'Hot Rod
Jalopy' respectively, again to avoid bans
for the reasons above. Johnny Cash's 'A
Boy Named Sue' was also censored at
the outset by the record company, to
avoid the hassle before it started. On the
Granada TV recording of Cash's 'San
Quentin' show, from which the record
was taken, the offering phrase is clearly
heard.

THE MOST BORING SEQUENCE OF ALBUM TITLES EVER

CHICAGO TRANSIT AUTHORITY
CHICAGO
CHICAGO 3
CHICAGO 4 – LIVE AT CARNEGIE HA
CHICAGO 5
CHICAGO 6
CHICAGO 7
CHICAGO 8
CHICAGO 9 – THEIR GREATEST HITS
CHICAGO 10

Guess who all these were by. Really, this
list speaks for itself. Most of them were
double or triple album sets, too . . .

TEN 'BIG' RECORDING ACTS

THE BIG BOPPER
BIG MAYBELLE
BIG MAMA THORNTON
BIG JIM SULLIVAN
BIG BOB KORNEGAY
BIG JAY McNEELY
ARTHUR 'BIG BOY' CRUDUP
BIG THREE
MR BIG
BIG BROTHER AND THE HOLDING COMPANY

While there are plenty of 'Littles' around in the rock world, it seems that 'Bigs' are harder to find (at least, we struggled a bit with the list above). The three group names at the end probably have no significance in the way of size; the Big Three were one of the most popular early Liverpool groups, and probably chose that name to emphasise the existing popularity of the three players (Brian Griffiths, John Gustafson and John Hutchinson) who came together to form it. Big Brother & The Holding Company were the band which featured the pre-solo Janis Joplin on lead vocals, while Mr Big were a successful UK group of the late 70s.

The individuals are all 'big' because they were – either in stature or girth! Arthur 'Big Boy' Crudup was a bluesman and one of Elvis Presley's early influences – he wrote and originally recorded 'That's All Right Mama', Presley's first single. Likewise, Big Mama Thornton had the original hit version of Presley's 'Hound Dog'. The others are also R&B performers of note, except for the Big Bopper, who is well-known, and Big Jim Sullivan, a British guitarist of more than 25 years standing as an in-demand session and backing group player. He has also occasionally recorded in his own right.

TEN 'LITTLE' RECORDING ARTISTS

LITTLE RICHARD
LITTLE WILLIE JOHN
LITTLE MILTON
LITTLE ANTHONY & THE IMPERIALS
LITTLE EVA
LITTLE JOHNNY TAYLOR
LITTLE JIMMY OSMOND
LITTLE SONNY
LITTLE TONY
LITTLE JIMMY DICKENS

Many of the above can probably attribute their name to diminutive stature, though Jimmy Osmond was also 'little' in the sense of being very young when he cut his non-classics like 'Long-Haired Lover From Liverpool'. R&B and blues artists strongly favoured the 'Little' tag; apart from Osmond and the last two on the list, all those here fit into a blues or soul bag. Little Tony was an Italian pop-rocker who had a UK hit with 'Too Good' in 1960, while Little Jimmy Dickens is a veteran country artist who gave the world the classic(?) 'May The Bird Of Paradise Fly Up Your Nose' in 1965.

Little Milton

THE LEAST SUCCESSFUL GROUPS EVER?

Obviously, the 'least success' is a completely unquantifiable concept. Significant non-success, however, involves the releasing of a lot of records without really ever selling many of them to anybody. It doesn't happen so much today, because nobody can afford to keep pushing a no-hoper for ever; groups lose their recording contracts, break up, move on. In the 1960s, however, when all was optimism and opportunism, anybody was willing to give a group a chance, or a dozen chances, to make it. Herewith, ten 60s groups with a whole bunch of flop records between them.

1 **ACTION**
(6 singles and a never-released album)
2 **EPISODE SIX**
(8 singles)
3 **EXECUTIVES**
(at least 9 singles)
4 **IAN & THE ZODIACS**
(7 singles; one album released only in the USA)
5 **GIBSONS**
(7 singles)
6 **ALAN BOWN SET**
(11 singles and an album)
7 **WINSTON G & THE WICKED**
(6 singles)
8 **ARTWOODS**
(7 singles, an EP and an LP)
9 **FLEUR DE LYS**
(7 singles)
10 **BEATSTALKERS**
(at least 8 singles)

There were many more cases of similar lengthy effort but non-achievement, of course. Just to prove that individuals can rise to greater heights when the groups give up the ghost, however, Episode Six spawned both Ian Gillan and Roger Glover, while Jon Lord and Keef Hartley emerged from the Artwoods.

TEN FORMER OCCUPATIONS

ELVIS PRESLEY – Truck Driver
BILLY JOEL – Boxer
DAVE CLARK – Film Stunt Man
CHUCK BERRY – Hairdresser
FRANK SINATRA – Sports Writer
MATT MONRO – Bus Driver
CARL PERKINS – Baker
CHRISSIE HYNDE – Rock Journalist
GRAHAM NASH – Assistant Manager of a Gents' Outfitters
BILL WITHERS – Toilet Seat Maker in an Aircraft Factory

Needless to say, none of them went back to a steady job. If the idea of Chuck Berry as a hairdresser boggles the mind slightly, let it be known that he actually holds a college diploma in the subject. Carl Perkins is a ranch owner nowadays when he's not out on the road, but no doubt he still turns out the odd mean loaf of bread. Elvis Presley drove trucks a few times in his movies, but was generally content in later years with Cadillacs and fast motorcycles. As for Bill Withers, he is not known to rest on his former laurels!

THE PERSONALITIES ON THE SLEEVE OF WINGS' 'BAND ON THE RUN' ALBUM

PAUL McCARTNEY
LINDA McCARTNEY
DENNY LAINE
KENNY LYNCH
CHRISTOPHER LEE
JAMES COBURN
MICHAEL PARKINSON
CLEMENT FREUD
JOHN CONTEH

Three singer/musicians, one wife, two actors, one TV chat show host, one Liberal Member of Parliament, and one former pro boxer! The sleeve pic is a still from a short movie of this oddly assorted cast actually acting out a 'band on the run' prison escape sequence, which Wings have had projected as a backdrop to their stage performances of the album title cut from time to time.

Quite how the personnel were chosen (and why) is worthy of speculation. The most likely explanation is that all were acquaintances of Paul McCartney, who agreed to take part just for kicks.

TEN INFAMOUS JONATHAN KING PSEUDONYMS

SAKKARIN
NEMO
SHAG
COUNT GIOVANNI DE REGINA
WEATHERMEN
BUBBLEROCK
53RD AND 3RD
100 TON AND A FEATHER
SOUND 9418
FATHER ABRAPHART & THE SMURPS

Hits under this loony collection of alter-egos included 'It's The Same Old Song', 'Sugar Sugar', 'The Sun Has Got His Hat On' and 'Lick A Smurp For Christmas (All Fall Down)'. King almost certainly holds the record for recording under the most different names and coming up with hits to boot. Only Count Giovanni De Regina with 'Just One Cornetto' (taken from the familiar TV ad to the melody of 'O Sole Mio') failed to make the British charts, from the selection of odd bods listed above.

Jonathan King

TEN CHARTMAKING TRIBUTE SONGS

Heinz

The making of a tribute record to a popular artist closely following that artist's death seems on the surface the quickest and sickest way to big money, but in fact most of the above selection were genuine celebrations of the talent of the chosen subject(s), and in many cases were made too long after the death concerned to be regarded as cashing in.

Several discs attempted to capture part of the sound of the act to which they were dedicated, notably those by Ronnie McDowell, Danny Mirror, Larry Cunningham and Heinz. The Johnny Cymbal and Righteous Brothers discs were concerned with a general catalogue of departed stars, rather than any particular artist, the latter song asserting that the rock'n'roll heaven must have 'a hell of a band'!

TRIBUTE TO BUDDY HOLLY
Mike Berry & The Outlaws
(Buddy Holly)

THREE STARS
Tommy Dee
(Buddy Holly, Big Bopper, Ritchie Valens)

THE KING IS GONE
Ronnie McDowell
(Elvis Presley)

I REMEMBER ELVIS PRESLEY
Danny Mirror
(Elvis Presley)

JUST LIKE EDDIE
Heinz
(Eddie Cochran)

TRIBUTE TO A KING
William Bell
(Otis Redding)

COLE, COOKE AND REDDING
Wilson Pickett
(Nat 'King' Cole, Sam Cooke, Otis Redding)

TRIBUTE TO JIM REEVES
Larry Cunningham & The Mighty Avons
(Jim Reeves)

TEENAGE HEAVEN
Johnny Cymbal
(several)

ROCK'N'ROLL HEAVEN
Righteous Brothers
(several)

TEN VERY LONG AND QUITE RIDICULOUS SONG TITLES

I'VE BEEN CARRYING A TORCH FOR YOU FOR SO LONG, IT'S BURNT A GREAT BIG HOLE IN MY HEART
Nino Tempo and April Stevens

DID YOU EVER SEE A DIVER KISS HIS WIFE WHILE THE BUBBLES BOUNCE ABOUT ABOVE THE WATER?
Shirley Ellis

THE INEXHAUSTIBLE QUEST FOR THE COSMIC CABBAGE
Ted Nugent

JEREMIAH PEABODY'S POLYUNSATURATED QUICK-DISSOLVING FAST-ACTING PLEASANT-TASTING GREEN AND PURPLE PILLS
Ray Stevens

THE ANAHEIM AZUSA AND CUCAMONGA SEWING CIRCLE, BOOK REVIEW AND TIMING ASSOCIATION
Jan And Dean

CLAUDE PELLIEU AND J.J. LEBEL
DISCUSS THE EARLY VERLAINE
BRAD BREAD CRUST FRAGMENTS
Fugs

COULD THE CHRISTIANS WAIT
FIVE MINUTES? – THE LIONS ARE
HAVING A DRAW
Man

SEVERAL SPECIES OF SMALL
FURRY ANIMALS GATHERED
TOGETHER IN A CAVE AND
GROOVING WITH A PICT
Pink Floyd

THE GREEN WITH ENVY, PURPLE
WITH PASSION, WHITE WITH ANGER,
SCARLET WITH FEVER, WHAT WERE
YOU DOIN'
IN HIS ARMS LAST NIGHT BLUES
Julie Rayne

SIR B. McKENZIE'S DAUGHTER'S
LAMENT FOR THE 77th MOUNTED
LANCERS' RETREAT FROM THE
STRAITS OF
LOCH KNOMBE IN THE YEAR OF OUR
LORD 1727, ON THE OCCASION OF
THE ANNOUNCEMENT OF HER
MARRIAGE TO THE LAIRD OF
KINLEAKIE
Fairport Convention

Nothing more needs to be said, except
that if even longer and more stupid song
titles do exist, the authors would be
delighted to hear about them.

Peter and Gordon

TEN HIT COVER VERSIONS OF BUDDY HOLLY SONGS

LOVE'S MADE A FOOL OF YOU
Crickets
TRUE LOVE WAYS
Peter And Gordon
NOT FADE AWAY
Rolling Stones
THAT'LL BE THE DAY
Everly Brothers
RAINING IN MY HEART
Leo Sayer
WELL ALL RIGHT
Santana
OH BOY
Mud
EVERYDAY
Don McLean
HEARTBEAT
Showaddywaddy
I'M GONNA LOVE YOU TOO
Hullaballoos

Ted Nugent

Scores of acts have revived songs from
the rich Buddy Holly song catalogue (the
Beatles, for instance, recorded 'Words Of
Love'), but all the above ten represent hit
singles in either America or Britain. Linda
Ronstadt's 'It Doesn't Matter Any More'
has been excluded because although
Holly recorded the original version of this
song, he didn't have a hand in writing it.

189

THE RAREST SINGLES AND ALBUMS

This is obviously something which it is impossible to list with any sort of authority, 'rare' being an almost unclassifiable concept. However, certain discs do keep being mentioned in discussion about rarity, and upon hopelessly hopeful wants list in collectors' magazines. Below is a sample of them.

1 **STORMY WEATHER**
   Five Sharps
2 **TV GUIDE PRESENTS ELVIS**
   Elvis Presley
3 **ELVIS AND JANIS (LP)**
   Elvis Presley & Janis Martin
4 **YESTERDAY AND TODAY (LP)**
   Beatles
5 **YOU AIN'T TREATING ME RIGHT**
   Mac Curtis
6 **ROLLING STONES PROMOTIONAL ALBUM**
   Rolling Stones
7 **WHO DID IT (LP)**
   The Who
8 **JOLLY WHAT! (LP)**
   Beatles and Frank Ifield
9 **MIDSUMMER NIGHT'S SCENE**
   John's Children
10 **PERFECT FOR PARTIES (EP)**
   Elvis Presley

Remember again that this is just a representative sample, and this list isn't necessarily in order of value, although you would expect to pay over £100 (well over, in some cases) for any item on this list at current British collector prices – always assuming you could find a copy for sale (the compilers have one of the albums above, but they're not saying which – and it's NOT for sale!)

'Yesterday And Today' by the Beatles is the version with the shunned, withdrawn and ostensibly destroyed 'butcher sleeve'; the standard sleeve version of the album is worth normal LP price. 'Elvis And Janis' was a rare ten-inch album issued only in South Africa, while 'TV Guide', 'Perfect For Parties' and the Stones album were all promotional-only ultra-limited editions. The Who album and John's Children (with Marc Bolan) single were withdrawn before official release, and only a few promo copies ever surfaced. The Mac Curtis single is an obscure mid-50s British release which is THE premium find for rockabilly collectors, and 'Jolly What' was a sort of compilation album put out in the States by Vee Jay records in 1963, featuring various tracks from early singles by Ifield and the Beatles. The sleeve proclaims that it was recorded on stage, but it's nothing of the sort. Finally, 'Stormy Weather', an R&B doo-wop single from 1952, is reckoned to be the rarest record in the world, since the pressing plant burnt down the night after the first batch were made, destroying all known copies plus the disc master, the tapes, the lot. A couple of advance copies which were taken out of the factory earlier that same evening have survived.

THE BEATLES AND FRANK IFIELD

The tremendous surging influence that has of recent months been felt by the Euro Recording artists has never before been equaled as in this album. Without any tion THE BEATLES and FRANK IFIELD are the most popular recording stars in E THE BEATLES are considered a phenomena on the American scene in that this is first time that a European base recording act has so captivated the American p from both TV and recording standpoint.

It is with a good deal of pride and pleasure that this copulation has been present

SIDE ONE
PLEASE, PLEASE ME
THE BEATLES
ANY TIME
FRANK IFIELD
LOVESICK BLUES
FRANK IFIELD
I'M SMILING NOW
FRANK IFIELD
NOBODY'S DARLING
FRANK IFIELD
FROM ME TO YOU
THE BEATLES

SIDE TWO
I REMEMBER YOU
FRANK IFIELD
ASK ME WHY
THE BEATLES
THANK YOU GIRL
THE BEATLES
THE WAYWARD WIND
FRANK IFIELD
UNCHAINED MELODY
FRANK IFIELD
I LISTEN TO MY HEART
FRANK IFIELD

VJLP 1095

VEE-JAY RECORDS

FAMOUS LAST WORDS

(or at least, words they later probably wished they'd never said)

JERRY LEE LEWIS, never a man noted for his modesty: **"I've never considered myself the greatest, but I'm the best."**

KEITH MOON, with sad irony in retrospect: **"I'm a victim of me own practical jokes."**

KAREN CARPENTER of the **CARPENTERS,** no doubt with some bitterness: **"The image we have would be impossible for Mickey Mouse to keep"**

Humble **MICK JAGGER: "I'm one of the best things England's got. Me and the Queen".**

Or if you want a transatlantic equivalent, how about **JOHN DENVER: "I epitomise America."**

NEIL YOUNG, not the steady family man type: **"You gotta keep changing – shirts, old ladies, whatever."**

WILLIE NELSON on why he decided he might as well be a Country superstar: **"I considered preaching, but preachers don't make a lot, and they work hard."**

RANDY NEWMAN, a man of few illusions: **"In a word, I'm boring."**

TED NUGENT, another humble self-effacer: **"I'm totally the product of my own desires; I have life dicked!"**

And the late **RITCHIE VALENS,** after winning the toss of a coin with **WAYLON JENNINGS** to see who would ride in the plane along with **BUDDY HOLLY** and **THE BIG BOPPER: "Gee, that's the first time I've ever won anything in my life!"**

Keith Moon

TEN LISTS WHICH WERE INTENDED FOR THIS BOOK, BUT REJECTED BY THE PUBLISHER!

During the course of preparing material for this book, the compilers produced many more lists, both factual and utterly trivial, than appear in the finished work. Our publisher, for reasons of lack of space or personal prejudice (and he isn't saying which apply to which lists!), handed a wad of them back to us among vague murmurings about 'Volume 2' Below we list ten of the categories which were rejected; who knows – if enough people are sufficiently intrigued by them to write to Virgin Books enquiring about 'Volume 2', perhaps you will someday be holding the full text of what is below in your hands, too!

1 **HIT SINGLES WITH RED INDIAN CONNECTIONS**
2 **ACTORS WHO HAVE PORTRAYED ROCK STARS IN MOVIES**
3 **THE FIRST COMMERCIAL RADIO STATIONS ON THE AIR**
4 **TOP TEN EQUESTRIAN SONGS**
5 **TEN HITS NAMED AFTER LONDON TUBE STATIONS**
6 **FOOTWEAR TOP TEN**
7 **ARTISTS AND GROUPS NAMED AFTER BIRDS AND ANIMALS**
8 **SONGS TITLED AFTER ALCOHOLIC DRINKS**
9 **SONGS TITLED AFTER NON-ALCOHOLIC DRINKS**
10 **CHARTMAKERS WITH THE SAME SURNAMES AS AMERICAN PRESIDENTS**

Look like winners, don't they?